Praise for *Living the Deeper YES*

"With hundreds of books pointing us in the same direction, Anna Huckabee Tull's *Living the Deeper Yes* stands out with its authentic voice, engaging stories, and wise counsel. Her deeply moving and personal journey will captivate you while her discerning and practical guidance for "Discovering the Finest, Truest Place Within You" will lead you to the answers and peace that we all want and have within us. Anna takes age-old wisdom and the best of contemporary psychology and offers a fresh, accessible, inspiring roadmap. I highly recommend it even for the seasoned traveler."

> —Robin Casarjian, Author of *Forgiveness: A Bold Choice for A Peaceful Heart*, Director of The Lionheart Foundation, Sponsor of the National Emotional Literacy Projects for Prisoners and Youth At-Risk

"Anna's book powerfully discloses an oft overlooked reality we are all faced with: *the entangled relationship we have with ourselves. Living the Deeper YES* mindfully teaches us how to *"unblend from the places inside that hurt."*

> —"Twinkle" Marie Manning, Editor of *Women of Spirit: Exploring Sacred Paths of Wisdom Keepers*

"Anna advises us to slow down, reframe our pain, and find ourselves amid life's distractions, until what was once almost invisible becomes a beautiful new lens through which you see your life and the world."

> —Tony Silbert, Author of *Healing Conversations Now*

"A captivating book written by one of the most introspective, courageous, go-get-'em people I've ever encountered. Anna is a force of nature."

> —Szifra Birke, Author of *Together We Heal* and Host of "Shrink Rap"

"Change and practice require a willingness to go into discomfort and often to suffer pain and confusion in order to come out the other side with more strength and ability. Anna hits this note again and again with such hopefulness and promise that the discomfort is transposed into an opportunity and gift you give yourself."

—Jay A. Livingston, M.A., Executive Coach and Author
of *Simple Steps to Change: Your Business, Your Life*

"A beautiful, powerful message—one that will help readers open up their lives in ways they have never imagined."

—Rebecca Lotenero, KN Literary Arts

"Anna is inviting you to step into the light, live in the light. And she's offering her hand, her wisdom, and her heart to you to be your guide and your companion on this journey. These words came to me in a dream the other night before I even finished her luminous and magical book, *Living the Deeper Yes*. I woke up and said to the dawn light, 'YES. Thanks, Anna.' Read her book and you will thank her, too."

—Dr. David C. Treadway, Author of *Intimacy, Change, and Other Therapeutic Mysteries*

"*Living the Deeper YES* is a wise, heartfelt guide to awakening to your full divine and human potential and a warm tribute to Anna Huckabee Tull's search for and mastery of her own Deeper YES. With the 'energetic playfulness' of her writing and clear, foundational concepts and steps, Anna draws people in as a wise, warm Presence handing the reader the keys to unlocking their own mysteries. This book is a deep dive that can't help but uplift the world."

—Drs. H. Ronald and Mary R. Hulnick, Authors of
Remembering the Light Within: A Course in Soul-Centered Living and *Loyalty to Your Soul: The Heart of Spiritual Psychology*, Cofounders and Directors of University of Santa Monica Programs in Spiritual Psychology

"Reading this book is like discovering you have a best friend (with whom you were in no way fully acquainted) talking to your heart from hers. She is boundlessly enthusiastic about you and your possibilities, she is deeply respectful ('I am bowing before the known and unknown that lie within you'), and she is a wise and insightful companion, who is happily sharing your journey and hers together.

"With Anna Huckabee Tull as your newest best friend speaking directly to *you* in this book, you can't help feeling cheered, championed, encouraged, and cherished—all at the same time. I warmly recommend

Living the Deeper YES to anyone who knows and needs the blessings of such a generous friend."
> —Richard Borofsky, Ed.D, Cofounder of The Center for the Study of Relationship and co-creator of *Marriage as a Spiritual Practice*

"Anna Huckabee Tull invites you to change your relationship with yourself, and if you take that invitation, you will encounter a completely different world. *Living the Deeper Yes* is a chart for navigating a journey that will take readers to new places of strength, acceptance, and beauty. And when the journey's done, they will find they have returned to their true, liberated selves."
> —Doug Hardy, Coauthor of *Monster Careers*

"An incredible book! So comprehensive and so chock-full of wisdom. The idea of a conversation with oneself, as Anna has formalized it here, is a momentous contribution to us all. I believe anyone who reads these pages will be empowered and softened at the same time."
> —Caitlin Selle, UU Reverence for Life Principal Member

"*Living the Deeper YES* has been huge in reinforcing my daily choice to tend to myself on a deeper level within."
> —Angela Renkoski, Founder of Divine Pattern Publishing and University of Santa Monica Graduate

"*Living the Deeper YES* is infused with Anna's flowing energy. It's the secret ingredient that will touch and inspire many, many readers."
> —Matteo Paris, Student of the Deeper YES

"Most of us know the fabulous feeling when we are living in the flow of our truest self. This book demonstrates how to get there, and how to stay there, to feel deeply good."
> —Rev. Dr. Jim Sherblom, Unitarian Universalist Minister and Author of *Spiritual Audacity*

**Also by Anna Huckabee Tull
(Musical Albums):**

Open Now

Other People's Stories

Love All Over the Place

Every Day

And, as a musical companion piece to the book
Living the Deeper YES:

The Days of Your Opening

Living the Deeper

YES

Discovering the Finest,
Truest Place Within You

ANNA HUCKABEE TULL

BALBOA
PRESS

A DIVISION OF HAY HOUSE

Excerpt from "The Invitation" from the book THE INVITATION by Oriah "Mountain Dreamer" House, © 1999. Published by HarperONE, San Francisco. All rights reserved. Presented with permission of the author www.oriah.org

This book is a work of non-fiction. Unless otherwise noted, the author and the publisher make no explicit guarantees as to the accuracy of the information contained in this book and in some cases, names of people and places have been altered to protect their privacy.

Balboa Press books may be ordered through booksellers or by contacting:

Balboa Press
A Division of Hay House
1663 Liberty Drive
Bloomington, IN 47403
www.balboapress.com
1 (877) 407-4847

Because of the dynamic nature of the Internet, any web addresses or links contained in this book may have changed since publication and may no longer be valid. The views expressed in this work are solely those of the author and do not necessarily reflect the views of the publisher, and the publisher hereby disclaims any responsibility for them.

The author of this book does not dispense medical advice or prescribe the use of any technique as a form of treatment for physical, emotional, or medical problems without the advice of a physician, either directly or indirectly. The intent of the author is only to offer information of a general nature to help you in your quest for emotional and spiritual well-being. In the event you use any of the information in this book for yourself, which is your constitutional right, the author and the publisher assume no responsibility for your actions.

Any people depicted in stock imagery provided by Thinkstock are models, and such images are being used for illustrative purposes only. Certain stock imagery © Thinkstock.

Print information available on the last page.

ISBN: 978-1-5043-7994-6 (sc)
ISBN: 978-1-5043-7996-0 (hc)
ISBN: 978-1-5043-7995-3 (e)

Library of Congress Control Number: 2017907236

Balboa Press rev. date: 07/14/2017

For the Younger Me,
who stumbled and lost her way.
This is everything I would have told you if I could.
This is everything we learned together, put to words.

And for Jim,
who has taught me about
looking farther, breathing deeper,
and the supreme power of loyalty mixed with love.

And for YOU,
in the earnest hope that you
set yourself free and
build something beautiful!

CONTENTS

SECTION 4 - NAVIGATE THE DEEPER YES
YOU IN MOTION

Foreword

Douglas Stone, Coauthor of *Difficult Conversations: How to Discuss What Matters Most,* Cofounder of Triad Consulting, and Lecturer at Harvard Law School

Anna knew what she was getting when she asked me to write this foreword. Or so I told myself as I fretted about just what to say. As friends and colleagues, we'd had long conversations during which I'd expressed my admiration for her work—and shared some of my doubts. Sure, I'd written some self-help books she'd liked, and Anna knows that I'm more open than some people to different ways of seeing the world. I'd been a guest on *Oprah* in 1999, and that stood as a significant overlap in our worlds—my "I'll believe it when I see it" view and Anna's view that "there's so much more to life than what we can see or even imagine."

I readily agreed to provide the foreword to this book because I know Anna. If *you* know Anna, then you know what *knowing* Anna means. Anna, in person, exudes a kind of magic, like a modern-day sorceress or wizard. She just knows things most people don't; she can give advice from an angle most people don't have access to. She'd helped me through some relationship challenges that, from where I stood, seemed insurmountable. She's (wildly) confident in herself, but more importantly, she's confident in *everyone*; you can't be in a room with her and not feel better about yourself than you did before she walked in. She's already been out past where you are and has returned to report back, in all her thrilling wide-eyed enthusiasm.

But what about Anna on the page? Could she energize and delight on the page as she does in person? Despite myself, or maybe because of myself, I was still skeptical.

So I started reading. I was immediately drawn in by the crackling energy of her writing, by the unique but relatable stories, by the empathy and soul. I was learning, I was feeling, I was moved and inspired. This should be enough for any reader, and yet about a third of the way through, I noticed a certain nagging doubt returning. An image came into my head: I am talking to Anna and we are having our usual conversation, the one where I tell her I'm open and interested but skeptical, and she smilingly reassures me there is so much more.

And then it happened: my imagined conversation with Anna merged precisely with what I was reading. At the end of a passage inviting the reader to try an introspective exercise, the book started to speak directly to me:

> "It's possible you are sensing a strong urge to find fault with this offering, to search for proof that your experience of it might be something less than amazing. But does this urge really serve you to the fullest? Or does it shield you—from failure, yes, but also, perhaps, from vulnerability, openness, potential, and success?"

Yes, book! This is exactly what I am thinking. Down this road lies the possibility of fulfillment, but also of vulnerability or failure. Is it possible that I am paralyzed by fear? Anna continues:

> "What if your resistant orientation ... is simply a form of fear?"

I think it is! But what should I do?!

> "And what if the antidote to that fear is its exact opposite? Fear's opposite, if you ask me, is not so much courage as it is *curiosity*. What might become possible for you ... if you allowed skepticism to give way, even for a short time, to curiosity? The answer lies within you. It lies within this exact moment, in which you decide to try this, or to fight against it."

That was all I needed to hear. The encouragement, yes, but more importantly, that Anna knew exactly what I was thinking, just as I was thinking it. This book about the miracle of uncovering and living in our most nourishing selves had produced a little miracle for me. I wanted proof that there is more to the world than I can see, and there it was, in the very words I was reading. Anna on the page was the next best thing to Anna in person, to having a conversation with the sorceress herself.

You may not be as skeptical as I was. But wherever you are is right where you're supposed to be. Anna will win you over as she won me, in person, on the page, or in whatever dimension you and she choose to meet.

Douglas Stone

Cambridge, Massachusetts, 2017

Introduction

From my parents I was given the gift of believing that anything is possible, as long as it is truly aligned with what your heart wants. The gift I hope to give you here is my very own grown-up, lived-into version of that exact same message:

Life is one repeating opportunity
to attune yourself to the stirrings of your heart
and then to dare to live into them.

I hope you find many things while reading this book, but I wish most of all to create, for you, these five in particular:

(1) I want to speak a language you long to hear.
I want to speak your language, only more so. I want to give voice to a way of communicating that resonates deeply within you. I want to put words on ideas that you did not ever quite realize there were words for, but when you hear them, they sound *right*.

(2) I want to get you thinking differently.
I want to get you thinking differently about what hurts, and what holds you back—about what you may be ready for, and what you are willing to try, now.

(3) I want to activate feelings you love to feel.
I want to activate within you a feeling of hopefulness. I long for you to feel awakened and newly alive in your own life as you engage with the ideas and anecdotes herein. I want to have chosen those ideas and anecdotes well, and timed them well, so that they leave you feeling *better*—not

because of the book you are reading but because of *the places within yourself that you are allowing to become activated* as you engage with these pages.

(4) I want to help you discover the finest, truest place within you.

I believe a place exists within your consciousness that will astound you. I want to help you become more familiar with this powerful seat of energy and to help you connect with this place from four easy angles, one for each section of this book, so that you can:

- **Shift the Balance** of your consciousness to incorporate more expansive and free-flowing energies into your life.

- **Change Your Mind** about upsets and drama—to discover how they are not meant to "knock you off balance" but rather to teach you when and how to turn inward.

- **Deepen the Conversation Within**, to help you build friendships with the places within you that most need attention, as *avenues toward* the places within you that hold the greatest concentration of clarity, wisdom, and forward momentum.

- **Navigate the Deeper YES**, to encourage you to steer your life from the seat of your strength and to move forward in ways that *feel deeply good.*

(5) I want to awaken your desire to play.

I want to present all of this material to you in a way that leaves you feeling playful about trying it on for size and then living into it. I want to help you develop an easy relationship with energetic shifts within yourself: ways of moving things around on the inside so that they feel better, so that your interactions with others feed you, and them, more and more fully.

Because that's it, really. We are gifted this one "wild and precious life," as the poet Mary Oliver so poignantly puts it. We can experience it partially. We can experience it from a place within ourselves that is pinched off or distant, fearful or resistant. Or we can dare to wake up and begin to ask:

What is my next step?
And how might it be amazing?

Q: What is the Deeper YES?

A: It is possibility and potential
waking up within you.

It's a concentration of energies
that are the seat of your power,
designed to snap into alignment
the moment you decide
to let it be so.

Will you?
Is it possible?
Shall we begin it now?

SECTION 1

SHIFT THE BALANCE

YOU AND LARGER ENERGIES

"The world is full of
magic things,
patiently waiting
for our senses
to grow sharper."

—*William Butler Yeats*

In this section, I intend to show you …

How you have probably been living
a smaller, more pinched-off version of
your life than you need to.

How the uphill battles
of your existence can melt away
when you tap into not just one but
two different levels of reality at the same time.

How harnessing the power of stopping
can help you invite much more
flow into your life.

How you can
SHIFT THE BALANCE
from a logistics-based to a
more essence-based orientation to life,
and in so doing,
discover a much more
buoyant and tapped-in
version of yourself.

Chapter 1

An Invitation

So, there you are.

You.

You and I are in no way fully acquainted. But meeting you here, I want you to know this: I am imagining myself, at the outset of our journey, bowing.

I am bowing before the known and the unknown that lie within you. And from deep within that bow, it is my great desire to reach out and connect. To connect with *you*, yes. But much more to the point, to connect with one very specific locus-point within you: **that place which represents your greatest concentration of clarity, focus, and joy**.

How might we help you access and activate that place, so that it can connect more directly with the world you live in? That's the journey of this book. I want to invite you to embrace the larger energies all around you, to transform the tangled and limiting stories of drama alive inside you, and to attune yourself to the voices within you that are wise and brave and can set you free into a life that feels deeply good. It starts with an invitation for you to follow me—not spellbound by any powers I might hold, but awakened and re-animated by your own. Because I want to invite you to take a peek at someplace amazing.

We are standing at the gateway and there it is before us: A Completely Different World of energies and possibilities—one that I have spent the last twenty years of my life learning to inhabit.

A COMPLETELY DIFFERENT WORLD

Look around and I will show you what I know about this Completely Different World. The energy of thought vibrates differently here. It has a robust power.

In this world, there is a palpable, positive connection between the thoughts you think and the events that play out around you. Here, your thoughts *interact* with what is occurring "out there." And what is occurring starts to *shift*, in ways that honor and favor you and those all around you.

You are gifted, here, with a powerful lens that allows you to see that some of the events playing out in your surroundings are offering you profound lessons, great clarity, and deep pleasure. And to see, too, that other events are truly not worthy of your attention. As temptingly as they may call out to you with their distraction, you, with your lens, can see beyond them, and they fall away.

You are different here, too. You know yourself as no one has ever known you. You are able to hear subtle messages from deep within yourself. Quiet, hidden messages of off-centeredness can be easily discerned. Intuitive, clarifying, expansive ideas and thoughts move forward in your consciousness in a way that allows you to easily *engage* them.

You are lighter here. You move about easily within the different levels and aspects of yourself. There is a playfulness about you—a tenderness, a strength. And bubbling up from within you like a fountain, there is joy.

And oh! So *much* is possible here. Possibility hangs ripe like fruit all around you. Not on every branch, but on so *many* of them! Your ability to discern which branches are most fruitful is such a clean, focused, intuitive ability. There is a knowing, here, deep within you, that your power is rooted in something larger than the confines of your own consciousness. You are *connected*. Tapped in. A vibrant life force moves through you, and you know yourself to be worthy of it. You know how to stay open to it. There is no place left in you that blocks this greater whoosh of energy-from-beyond. You are an open portal, and this energy flows through you: deeply, easily, magically.

In this Completely Different World, you can see the pain of others, beneath whatever pleasant or angry mask they hide it with. You can see the potential of others, even when they have lost sight of it themselves. In this world, you are grateful, growing, learning, expanding, expressing, and discerning. You are wise, trusted, and very present. You are unencumbered. You are *fun*. You are *good*. You are imperfect, but learning, humble, brave. And you are filled with a sense of experimentation and play.

On bad days, a world like this seems an eternity away—entirely out of reach. A fabrication. Some half-baked, unreachable version of perfection. Some drug trip, which sounds fabulous except that reality, dense and demanding, will always be waiting on the other side. This Completely Different World is just a life meant for some saint, or some other lucky bastard who had it better, had it easier, got handed something that you don't have. Someone, perhaps, who has not sustained the betrayals and disappointments of your particular life.

On dark days, in dark years, it is often all you can muster to just keep going. There is no Completely Different World like this. And if there is, you are locked out of it. Maybe it's someplace you get to go to when you die. But right now, there are bills to pay, arguments to kick up or run from, and more disappointments hovering just out of sight.

I don't have time for this, I hear you say. *Can't you see how busy I am? How far behind I have fallen? Take your poetry and your quiet moments in the woods and your tender eye gazes somewhere else. That's not where I am.*

And perhaps this is exactly the point.

I want to invite you to enter a Completely Different World that is located just exactly where you find yourself sitting in this one, particular moment.

I want to invite you to enter into this Completely Different World that exists, elusively, right where you are, even if entry is not easy at first. Even if it taxes your understanding of where you are and what is possible. I want to invite you to enter into this world because *you have been here before.* Maybe you've written it off as a temporary place—a moment of grace, some kind of random and fleeting good luck, a strange coincidence, or a mistake.

But it's no mistake.

I want to invite you into a place, right here, right now, where there is an expansiveness inside of you that is astonishing. Where the world around you reflects back to you the very best of who you are and always have been. I want to invite you into this world despite any resistance you might currently have or any limiting beliefs you might hold about your deserving to be here.

You deserve to exist in *this* version of reality. You are fully equipped to be here.

And getting a-a-a-a-a-l-l the way to this place, from wherever you currently find yourself stranded, begins, really, with engaging with an incredibly basic concept:

That "Completely Different World" already exists within your consciousness.

It's not a matter of my talking you into it, shaming you into it, or hijacking you and dragging you to this place to prove that it is real. It's simply a matter of locating it within your consciousness and interacting with it.

This is true even if this place is buried under piles of hurts, resentments, misunderstandings, and misinterpretations of reality.

There are *countless* ways of accessing this Completely Different World. There are luck-based ways. There are "random moment of grace"-type ways. There are ways of literally bumbling in "by mistake" on your way to something else. (*Oops! What? That moment right there was awesome! Wait! Where did it go?*) And there are plenty of ways that have to do with catastrophes and losses of epic and soul-wrenching proportions that crack you wide open and force you to learn to navigate anew.

But by far my favorite way, and the one I have dedicated my career to understanding, as I have made a lifetime study of *the Dynamics of Stuckness and Flow*, is by *learning how to shift your consciousness*. To, in essence, CHANGE YOUR MIND about what is possible.

It is largely an internal journey, though it's punctuated by all kinds of real-world evidence, once you are ready to see that evidence. And it has, at its root, the most fundamental relationship, friendship, and love affair that you will ever cultivate:

The key to that "Completely Different World" is your relationship with yourself.

I have come to believe, with a conviction deep and powerful, that the quality of essentially *everything* that plays out in your life has EVERYTHING to do with the nature of your own relationship with yourself—with how much you relate to *all* the different levels and facets of Who You Truly Are.

The sweetness of your interactions with yourself—the integrity, lightness, or heaviness of your interactions with yourself—is directly correlated to the sweetness and integrity and lightness or heaviness of the interactions you are able to attract and create out in the world.

The playfulness of your interactions with yourself—the creativity of your interactions with yourself, the judgmental-ness of your interactions with yourself, or, conversely, your ability to feel compassion for yourself, to encourage yourself, to draw clean boundaries within yourself—has EVERYTHING to do with your ability, out in the world, to engage on these same levels with others.

All of it, all of it, *all of it*, begins INSIDE HERE, in the Story of You, and in the way that you, consciously or unconsciously, relate to yourself. How you tune out, or tune in, to the messages coming from deep within you. How you trust or doubt those messages. And how, if you become disconnected from those deeper inner messages, you go about re-connecting.

I want to invite you into a space where you are so connected to yourself, so supportive of yourself from within, that The Brightness blooms and dances all around you, and The Darkness becomes simply an invitation to shine your light.

Your life is offering you a very specific invitation. And I am now inviting you to translate that invitation into something you can hear, work with, and benefit from.

The particular pathway that I am about to show you is all about the powerful, mind-bending, life-expanding things that can happen when you learn what it truly means to deepen your connection with yourself, and in so doing, deepen your connection with the people and energies all around you.

The place where this other world is, is right here. In your very skin. In this exact moment, whether the moment happens to appear, on the outside, to be filled with beautiful gardens or some new tax form arriving in your in-box. What is happening "out there" need not set the tone for what is happening, "in here," inside of you. The pathway I want to show you—the pathway I believe you, specifically, showed up here to learn about—starts right here, in this very instant.

Because this moment, always, is the portal to the place where the freest, sweetest, wisest, bravest, most generous version of you resides.

Chapter 2

A Second, Stronger Voice Within Us

Rose came to me deep into the most painful, unhinged year of her life. Upon hearing that I wrote songs on commission, she'd had a clear and powerful thought, rising up in stark contrast to the internal chaos she was feeling daily: *I want Anna to create a song for me! I want to hear this song and know that it is my own voice, calling me forward, helping me to move out of this pain and into something truer and more expansive.*

We sat down for a song interview. Rose was hunched over and small, almost keening on my couch. She talked about her terrible year—how her husband had left her, revealing a four-year affair, and had moved on immediately to wed this new partner, despite their 32-year marriage and a family complete with three lovely, grown daughters. Like many before her who have invited me to create a song for them, Rose was candid, brave, intelligent, and vulnerable in her sharing. But unlike anyone before her, practically every word out of her mouth sounded and felt too toxic to use in a forward-calling song. I watched her veer back and forth erratically between two states of being.

On the one hand: *I am so angry at him! How could he do this? I trusted him. My life is ruined! He is awful!*

And on the other: *I loved him so much. How could I have missed how hurting and lonely he must have been? What was it about me that made me so undesirable? How did I get so far removed from being attuned to what was going on in his world? I am awful!*

She was filled with tears and confusion, careening back and forth between furious and desperate states of mind. I tracked her every comment. I took fourteen pages of notes—a new record. Yet almost

7

every word seemed to tug her in an energetic direction that felt weak, lost, victimized, small, unguided. She spoke of deep, piercing wounds, of confusion and disappointment. Almost nothing in the vibrations of what she said sounded to me like a deeper, more authentic voice of self-rescue or possibility.

Except …

Except that five times, for the most fleeting of moments, when she opened her mouth, what came forward was of a different vibration entirely. Hidden among that embattled pushing and pulling, it turned out, were five extractable, twinkling gems. These fleeting comments just seemed to come from someplace "other"—someplace within her that was strong and brave, ready to rise up and shake itself off. Ready to begin anew and embrace a hopeful, forward direction.

"Some part of me knows that I have always known where I am going," she said, and I sat there, captivated. This caught my attention. But the next thing that came out of her mouth was more bile. "I am so sick of how stuck I feel," she said. Then: "I hear some voice deep within me, calling out to me," she said, but did not continue to follow the thread. Much later: "I know it's time to rise up to my full height," she said. And later still, after a review of her husband's many transgressions and her own shortcomings: "I just want to be able to truly stand in my own skin."

After another half-hour of complaints and self-doubt, rather astonishingly, she said one of the purest, most powerful things I had yet heard anyone say, in a song interview or anywhere else:

"I want to make peace within myself."

This idea was almost lost there, among all the upset, drama, and negativity.

What was this other voice? Whose was it? Where was it coming from?

A SECOND LEVEL OF REALITY

My journey has taught me that this voice, this vibration, this perspective of centeredness, even in an overwhelming situation, represents a second, co-existing level of reality. This deeper level, I have come to know, is always in existence, even in the darkest and most painful of times.

The story of Rose has an interesting and instructive ending. I did, in fact, toss almost everything she said onto the cutting room floor. I salvaged only the five things she had said that sounded like they were coming from a different, higher plane of reality within her, and I expanded them into a song. I invited Rose back to my house to hear it and, listening to it for the first time, tears of recognition streamed down her face. She expressed amazement that these were HER words. That they had been freed up from the muck they had been mired in and woven into something beautiful and inspiring.

After listening to the song, Rose went on her way.

Three months later, when the song had been studio-recorded, I opened the door and there on my front porch stood a woman I barely recognized: tall, radiant, suntanned, and vibrant. It took me a moment to realize that this was indeed Rose. She looked easily twenty years younger and four inches taller! But more to the point, she was so clearly alive, engaged, present … *happy.*

I invited her in, preparing her to hear the finished studio version of the song, but felt compelled to ask about the striking shift in her countenance. And that's when she explained to me what she had been doing for the past three months. Since I had last seen her, she had been listening to the rough-cut, homemade recording I'd given her, over and over and over.

"I listen to it all the time," she said. "This is my voice. I know this is my voice, singing directly to me. I can hear that this is my truth. It is changing me, to be able to clearly hear it."

The song, "Beauty in Me," when I shared it on the Internet, brought forward a similar reaction from innumerable other listeners, many of whom have written me to say, "I feel like this was created just for me." And I am not surprised.

I'm not surprised because the language of this "other voice," the vibration of it, the essence of what it is all about, is familiar to all of us.

I believe we all came here knowing about this "other voice" within us, and that, in fact, the moments where we are conscious of it and connected to it are among the finest moments of our time here on earth. Conversely, the moments in which we lose connection with it—forget what it means to honor that place within us that *knows*—are the moments we experience as dark, foreign, haunting, daunting, and most overwhelming.

It is my experience that there are genuinely two different levels of reality, and that, deep within us, we all actually know this. But it can just seem too strange to talk about it, most of the time.

But let's do. Let's look more carefully at the nuts and the bolts of this other level, and the voices within us that reach out to us from that place.

Chapter 3

Logistical Reality and Essence Reality

I began understanding this second "voice" twenty years ago when I started considering the dynamics of real-life Stuckness and Flow. In my work as a Life Coach, I had access to a long line of kind, interesting folks with lives that were flowing energetically in most ways, but frustratingly stuck in one area in particular (*my unorganized office, my love life, my job satisfaction, my mother*). To my delight and their relief, I was regularly able to help clients shift from stuck to un-stuck, with generally excellent results. But how? What was I really doing?

STUCKNESS AND FLOW AS A "WAY IN"

It started to dawn on me that when my clients looked at their stuckness, they saw only stuckness. When *I* looked at it, I too was able to see the stuckness (which helped with my ability to be empathetic). But unlike them, I was also, *simultaneously*, able to look at their "stuckness" and see ... flow. I was seeing some other realm, it seemed, where more was possible.

It was as though they were seeing one level of reality ("this can't work") and I was seeing two levels of reality ("this can't work" and, simultaneously, "this can work.") Their focus was rather singularly on the stuckness. *My* focus, on their behalf, took in both but seemed to be much more heavily tilted toward FLOW. For them, being in the presence of someone who could see FLOW, where they could not, felt energizing, hopeful, and uplifting. And from there, things started to change for them, for the better.

Fascinated, I pondered this: On the one level—on this "flowing" energetic level (or "completely different world") that I was seeing—whatever it was—*things never seemed to get stuck.* There was always another option, another perspective, another direction, and a sense of hope.

On the other, more logistical level—*job, relationship, challenging goal*—things flowed sometimes but got very stuck other times.

There are two levels. Energy flows consistently on the one level and sporadically on the other, I observed.

Even so, clients' stuck energies started to un-stick whenever they were re-connected with this "flowing" other level of energy that I was somehow able to see, even when they could not. More and more clients seemed to be seeking me out. This "other flowing level" seemed to be a huge part of why.

I began to make lists.

THE ENERGY OF STUCKNESS:

- Trying hard, making little progress
- Frustration, in over your head
- Longing to engage but resisting, procrastinating
- Distracting yourself with "easier," non-essential tasks
- Feeling trapped—all options seem paltry and undesirable
- Stagnant, bored, unengaged, lethargic
- Beating up on yourself: "I'm doing too little/too much; I'm doing it wrong"
- Fixating on, berating, or blaming others as the cause of your stuckness
- A general sense of "NO ..."

THE ENERGY OF FLOW:

- Ease, confidence, lightness, joy
- A sense of abundance and possibility
- The natural presence of hope, engagement, anticipation
- Playful experiments to learn and increase clarity
- A satisfying intersection of peace and invigoration
- A general sense of "YES!"

Stuckness, then, as I thought about it, looks something like this:

When stuckness in some particular area happens to me, it becomes hard to see beyond the confines of my dilemma. I feel small, solely focused on myself and, most specifically, on my pain or discomfort. If I have cut my toe, the world shrinks down to me, and the throbbing, and my toe. If I am fearful that I am about to lose my job, or a friendship, or about contracting a life-threatening illness, the world shrinks down to me, and my fear, and the way in which that fear is moving through me, rapidly painting vivid tableaus of worst-case scenarios. When it happens to me, I become a very "small package"—all wrapped up in myself and my woes.

In such a state, if a Completely Different World appears to me at all, it appears as someplace *"waaaaay* over there." If you've ever experienced depression, even fleetingly, you can relate to the experience of a full and vibrant "world" of engaged others playing out—painfully—seemingly VERY separate from the "world" you inhabit.

Even when the physical distance is nonexistent, the emotional, spiritual, and psychological distance can feel staggeringly, sometimes impossibly, unnavigable.

NOT SO FAR APART

But what if those two states of being are not as far apart as they seem? I began to wonder. Maybe part of what makes shifting from stuckness into flow *appear* so challenging is that we limit ourselves with the assumption that stuckness is one level—and flow is another one, far, far away. *Maybe these levels actually touch,* I thought. Maybe the more flowing level is

13

one simple shift in consciousness away, all the time. If only we could know how that's done …

This was an exciting concept. I started referring to the two levels as the **Logistical Level** and the **Essence Level**. I didn't quite have a definition for them yet, but it began to dawn on me that the Logistical Level seemed to be a "default" location for most of us—the place our consciousness stayed oriented toward, most of the time. There we were, running errands, making plans, sticking to or breaking agreements. And then every once in a while, for reasons we could not quite fathom, we would POP into this deeper, more flowing place.

Maybe we pop to this place because <u>it is right there</u>. Maybe this place is easier to get to than we realize, if only we could tap into knowing how. If only this other way of being didn't seem to always appear "fleetingly" or "by mistake" or "out of the blue."

Maybe *everything* that happens on the Logistical Level—with our experiences, the pain we feel, our ability to learn from these experiences— is *leading* us to the Essence Level, if only we could see it. I began to lean into this strange idea because it excited me:

The events that play out on the Logistical Level are *always* leading us someplace deeper.

I could feel in my bones that I was onto something. Stirring, deep within me, a new awareness and an old remembrance seemed to be merging. I felt newly alert to the world around me. *Logistical and Essence MUST be connected instead of separate*, I thought to myself, heart pounding. But even so, *something* was nagging at me. And it wasn't until I was sitting with Rose at the song interview that it started to come together.

THE EVER-PRESENT WORLD OF ESSENCE

Rose and I were deep into our meeting. We were talking about how she felt marooned, apart, separate. I hopped up suddenly out of my chair and I found myself "demonstrating" in 3-D how I wanted to create a song for her that made it possible to make a leap from HERE (the red Turkish rug in my living room, which, I suggested, represented the place where she was stuck, in the Logistical World—picking up the pieces, having to start over, alone, dealt out of all the critical conversations and decision-making)—to HERE (the smooth, shining wood of our floors, which, I enthused, could represent the Essence Level—the world of feeling clear and certain, navigating from within, rising up in the face of change, and inviting that change to deepen and strengthen her).

Back and forth I danced and leapt: You're way over HERE (rug)! We want to get you (leap) to HERE (floor)! We want a song that gives you the courage to make the necessary leap. I jumped back: HERE is where you are (rug). I leapt again: HERE is where we can help you go (wood)!

I thought about all my training, in energy work, in the basic tenets of Spiritual Psychology. I thought about everything I knew about the dynamics of stuckness and the dynamics of flow. I thought about all the times participants had commented to me over the years that they found it so remarkable that I seemed to be able to LEAP from one state of being to another, with ease, authenticity, and grace. I thought about how, over the years, in teaching courses, in assisting individuals, I have come to be known for modeling this, more than almost any other thing. And I wondered, how is it that I can leap so directly from one state to another within myself? And how is it that I can leap directly into someone else's "wavelength"—completely outside my own experience—in my Life Coaching practice and in my commissioned songwriting? How am I so able to navigate from stuckness to flow? From NO to YES? From a Logistical Orientation to an Essence Orientation?

What is it I know, that I don't <u>know</u> that I know?

I asked myself this question. It percolated. I kept working on Rose's song. The finished song moved her. It all worked. That should be enough.

But in the aftermath, I continued to think about myself jumping back and forth: Rug, Wood, Rug, Wood; Logistical, Essence, Logistical, Essence. And finally it hit me. It hit me what it is that I know: what kind of knowing I incorporate, so very much of the time, regardless of whether I am standing on the rug (Logistical) OR on the wood (Essence).

There is wood under that rug.

My living room is not a freak-of-nature location, where you lift up the rug and there is nothing but a black hole reaching forever into some endless non-eternity.

There is wood under that rug.

There is Essence Level energy *underneath* Logistical Level energy. All the time. The Logistical Level is not some separate reality floating out in the middle of nothing. Essence energy is under there—part of the total picture, touching it, informing it, connecting to it—*in an ongoing way.*

When we are hurting, when we are small, when we are all wrapped up and trapped within our assumed dead-ends and lack of options, we forget—we FORGET—that there is wood under our rug. We forget that even if we can't see it, can't sense it, there is another powerful, positive level of reality that is touching our Logistical reality, and reaching out far beyond it as well.

THE LOGISTICAL REALITY *YOU DO SEE* → ← THE ESSENCE REALITY *YOU DON'T SEE*

If it's a rug we're talking about, there is a wood floor under there whether we think about it consciously or not. We can knock on the rug and feel the wood. If it's the Logistical Level we're talking about, *there are things we can do to re-connect with our knowledge of the Essence Level.* There are places we can stand, and people we can invite in—thoughts we can think, and thoughts we can release. When we do those things, this Essence Level can come more and more into the forefront of our consciousness.

When that happens, we can create a life that feels more authentic, more true to Who We Truly Are. More vibrant. More brave. More like a Deeper YES. It was starting to come clearer to me now:

Between the Essence Level and the Logistical Level, there is only the illusion of distance.

This idea that there is a long distance to travel between stuckness and flow is a limiting interpretation of reality. "Argue for your limitations," the author Richard Bach used to say, "and sure enough, they're yours."

When we stop arguing for limitations, we get to move about more freely, from a deeper place within us.

So what about you?

I believe a second "reality" is present and part of your experience, right this minute, whether your consciousness is cued in to it or not.

I believe that when you lift up your eyes to see it (I will help you understand how this is done, piece by piece), you can discover that every inch of your Logistical reality is connected, at all times, to this other reality that is filled with so much more—like the way the wood is right there holding you up, even when you are so busy giving the credit to the rug. Like the way the sunlight can come pouring into your window on even the cloudiest of days, if you are sitting on an airplane, and soaring above the cloud cover.

The difference between the reality you may be heavily cued into right now and the gorgeous reality that may be invisible to you much of the time is simply the difference between a Logistical Orientation to the concrete world around you and an Essence Orientation to the life-affirming energy that surrounds you, at all times, on all levels.

LOGISTICAL AND ESSENCE: A COMPARISON

Let's flesh out these two levels of reality and discover how new possibilities—wondrous possibilities—can start to arise when you allow for a conscious interplay between the two.

The Logistical Level is the level we associate with and consciously choose to interact with, most of the time. It is the world of clocks, deadlines, and calendars. It is a level of reality that is largely knowable, measurable, and concrete. It's the science of temperature change. It's the predictability of the seasons. And, too, it's the predictability that if you say something unkind to someone, there is a good chance they will say something unkind back. It is the drama of emotional reactions to the events playing out around us. It's the world we see represented on TV and in the movies, most of the time, filled with witty banter, quick comebacks, humor, and gripping sagas. It's the parking ticket on your windshield, the items on your to-do list, and the food in your grocery bag. It's friendships and betrayals, councils and courtrooms, craft fairs and classrooms all over the planet. It's the world of items and emotions and events. It is, in short, Life As We Know It.

The Essence Level is something *entirely different*. It's the glorious magic of looking deeply into the eyes of one you hold dear. It's the serendipity of confluence, luck, and a sense of wonder. It's an intuitive wisdom and knowingness, deep within you. It's the splendor of the heavens and the way that looking up at a wide and twinkling sky can calm and expand you—cares falling away and truths taking on a new clarity. It's that powerful and sudden shift you experience when, in a flash, a new awareness suddenly comes over you. It's the AHA! It's the *Eureka!* It's that moment of profound fulfillment, when you relax into all that surrounds you, realizing, in that moment, that you want for nothing. It's experiencing the presence (*could it be?*) of a loved one who has passed on and yet, somehow, even so, is right there with you in the room. This level is all about the synchronicities of timing and the small miracles of beauty and coincidence that surprise and delight us. It's the domain of imagination, of play, of creating something where before there was nothing but the germ of an idea. It is the wavelength of possibility.

These two levels are very different. I can look up and see the sun, from the Logistical Level, and I can think, "Oh my gosh, it's about to get dark. I'm running late." I can look up at the sun, from the Essence Level, and see a brilliant array of pinks and purples melting before me, feeling myself expand, breathe more deeply, and flow into this moment. It's the same sun I'm looking at, but I can view it from two very different "worlds" within myself.

I remember an early Essence Level "snap in" moment happening for me once, long ago, in (of all places) a bowling alley. There I was, gutter-balling away with friends when suddenly something stunning occurred within me. I was overtaken by a profound shift. I had drawn back my arm and before I had even released the ball, deep within the fullness of my being, I *knew* and could feel with absolute clarity that this ball, this swing, had already knocked all the pins down. I *knew* this, even though, on the Logistical Level, the ball had not yet left my hand.

And so it was.

Sure enough: Whoosh! Pop! In all directions, those pins scattered in the powerful explosion of a strike.

I had surprised myself by hitting strikes before and I have since, but this was something different.

Everything about this moment felt entirely owned by me. I was fully standing, moving, swinging, and existing from a place within me that was somehow unlimited by any notion that I might not be fully aligned with what I was doing.

Moments like these are as significant for what is absent from them as for what is present within them:

- Present: clarity, confidence, ease, certainty, joy, presence, attunement, awareness, flow.
- Absent: doubt, worry, fear, worst-case scenarios, embarrassment, negative self-talk, concern, judgment, upset, second-guessing, blame, drama.

THE SUDDEN SHIFT INTO ESSENCE

I had bumbled (or *seemingly* bumbled) my way into plenty of similar moments of ease and wonder at many other junctures in my early days along this path:

- Grieving the oh-so-recent death of my grandmother, feeling an unspeakable tightness in my heart and throat, and then—whoosh— as smooth and certain as if she were there, kissing my brow, feeling soothed and centered and completely released of the ache ...
- A moment alone, traveling out West, where my gaze landed upon one singular tree and suddenly I *saw* that tree, and felt it communing with me. I could feel its vibrancy and energy infusing me, weaving some pattern into my own as I blinked away surprised tears ...
- Seeing a lone dancer dressed all in white in a Spanish-speaking church in a rough neighborhood outside of Boston, where I knew no one. Watching her, transfixed, until I forgot where I was. *I am part of it. I am beyond myself. She is inside the dance and I am right there with her.*

How is it that all of us have at some point experienced transcendent moments like these and yet so many of us do not understand how such a moment came to be?

What keeps us from becoming more curious about that? Inviting more of that in? Is it really fully random? Does our presence, the level of our consciousness, have nothing to do with full, glorious moments such as these coming to pass?

For me, early on this path to "incorporating more Essence," I felt as if moments like this "happened to" me. They seemed to appear, unexpectedly, unbidden, from out of nowhere. They felt like luck, not something I knew would repeat, and certainly nothing that would have occurred to me to invite or "conjure," or believe that I could.

Many people call such moments "spiritual experiences," assuming most of our life is NOT a spiritual experience until occasionally, fleetingly, we have one.

But as my own life began to shift, I started to deeply ponder a concept put forth by the philosopher Pierre Teilhard de Chardin. What if we are not, in fact, human beings occasionally having a spiritual experience? What if, instead, we are *spirits having a human experience?*

For me, this has turned out to be a radical, life-expanding concept.

What if the Essence of who I am is something much, much larger than this body that I have been born into? What if the truth of Who I Am becomes dramatically limited—pinched off—in each moment that I align myself too closely with the Logistical World?

I asked myself: *What if living life deeply aligned with the Logistical World means that I am making choices and reinforcing "realities" that keep me small and make it harder to connect with the place within me that knows that there is, on some other level, much more that is available to me?*

And what would it mean, in practical terms, to lift my head up and not only see this second level but begin to interact with it more consciously?

But how is this done? I wondered. Is this something I might be able to invite, rather than simply watching in awe when it happens? And if I am able to choose it, how might I continue to interact with it, once I have called it forward?

Chapter 4

The Power of Stopping

In my experience, tapping into the Essence Level is *not* something that happens because you try really hard.

It is not a connection you can scold or shame yourself into making, or talk yourself into seeing by squinting fiercely and concentrating.

It is not a function of how much you did or did not go to church as a child, or how much money you have donated to charities in the previous fiscal year. And the Essence Level is not some reward, distantly waving at you through the heat like a mirage on the other side of your shining, completed To Do list.

That said, it is also not anywhere near as elusive or exclusive or unreachable as it may seem. It is, in fact, all-pervasive, available at every turn, in the most exalted of moments, and at the most bitter and contaminated instances of disappointment.

The entry point to the Essence Level is ... *stopping*.

Flow begins to happen when you stop thinking, when you stop feeding-feeding-feeding that connection to the Logistical Level.

Access to the Essence Level is YOU, here, now, breathing into wanting access. And then feeling the tiny *shiver* of an opening within you. For deeper energies to emerge and align, the more superficial energies must be stilled.

It's you, in this moment, arrested, mid-motion from whatever urgent, agenda-filled vector you were on.

It's you, stopping what you are doing, then slowing the pace of your mind to feel the wonder, sweetness, and love of the world.

I learned about the power of stopping the hard way.

A FORCED STOP

When I was thirty years old, life invited me to stop. My entire situation suddenly ground itself down to a halt.

I know it now, though I didn't know it then: Lives sometimes do this, when the live-er of the life has used up all there is of an old system, an old way of understanding *Who I am* and *What is possible.* Sometimes life says to you, "You are at the end of the line for this way of being. It's non-negotiable and this phase is over." That's what my experience felt like. I didn't plan a shutdown. One simply inserted itself into my story. And when it did, it seemed and felt like the worst thing that had ever happened to me.

I am happily married now, in a deep and very authentic-feeling way. I was married once before, though the good feelings I found in that situation were based on something far less sturdy within me, and far more fleeting.

That time around, it was an intense and secretive courtship. I felt unleashed and alive in some strange new way. The relationship was all and everything for a time—so engrossing and absorbing that I came to believe that, were this powerful connection ever to be ripped away, it would surely be the end of me.

It came to seem as if there were nothing more valuable in my life than this one powerful bond with this one particular person, and that literally *anything* else in my life was worth sacrificing, if need be, in order to keep this intense experience afloat. When I tried to picture any life out beyond that marriage, were it to end (and I did sometimes contemplate this, after particularly dizzying fights), the most I could come up with was an ill-conceived image of myself crawling back home to my parents' house in Ohio and living out my days lying on a makeshift bed in their basement. (I know. I hear myself.)

In that imaginary iteration, my parents would wobble down the decrepit stairs into their dimly lit, unfinished basement to regularly bring me food. I hadn't really thought through the whole *"there is no bathroom in the basement"* part. The tableau was clearly not one I had explored thoroughly. It was just a hasty vision of the end of the line: who I would be if I were no longer loved by this one particular man in this one particular way—if the intense union we had thrown ourselves into—which made me feel so free and above it all—somehow slipped away from my clutches.

From here, of course, I can see it: The breakup of that marriage was the catalyst for the most significant and far-reaching shift of my life. My eventual ability to look back at what had happened—to ponder what I had built and why it had filled me up so fast yet disintegrated so quickly— brought about a life-arc course correction of profound proportions. But at the time, the breakup was simply everything I had feared coming to pass.

Things happened fast. Or at least, I didn't notice that something seemed to have completely sputtered out and then, suddenly, irrevocably, I did. *Everything*, it seemed, ended all at once. The breaking apart of us felt cosmic to me on one level and decimating on another. The threads of connection we had once so fully felt seemed utterly unavailable.

There was a shaking, disassembling feeling of all the bonding pieces sliding away and nothing at all to replace them with. My home, my job, my in-laws, the state that we had so recently relocated to, the business we had so recently picked up the reins on together—all of it was connected to him. This unforeseen about-face in connection knocked me edgewise like absolutely nothing before.

Which is how I found myself, suddenly, at the end of the line. Stopped. Everything in my life had abruptly and simultaneously ceased.

I had no more ability to keep navigating in the way that I had been. No more desperately stepping forward, asking everything around me to bow in service to my singular goal of keeping myself on that sinking raft—a raft that, surely, felt sink-ish to him, too. Gone, suddenly, was the obsession to hang on at all—an obsession that had made me, increasingly, un-centered, unattractive, uninteresting, unrecognizable. To those around me. To this partner who had lost interest. And to myself.

Here was the arrival of the worst thing ever—the thing I had dreaded, the thing I had done everything imaginable, in my own mind, to keep from coming to pass. And it *was*, as I had feared, BAD. I did go back to my parents' house, driving all the way from Texas to Ohio, sobbing, speeding, puffy-faced and despondent. (They gave me the guest room, so the basement nightmare, at least, was avoided.) I was out of work. I had no home. I had no plans. I had no vision for anything that might lie on the other side of this whirlwind that could possibly have any value at all. I was heartsick and sad and weepy and *a mess*.

One moment it had been all systems go: I was fully engaged in building a Logistical Level construction based on Logistical Level thinking: *If the two of us could just hold on tight enough and keep moving fast enough, whatever it was that we had could be kept in motion, and all the demons of our un-communicated thoughts and fears could be held at bay indefinitely. Surely. Surely.*

The next moment, all of it was gone, as if it had only been a dream in the first place.

On my last bit of steam, I made it to that guest room bed at my parents' house, flopped weakly down upon it, pulled a sheet over my face, and promptly stopped being or doing anything.

Motion arrested.

It is not until we stop scurrying forward that we can begin to hear the new energies rising up within us.

From that stock-still position under the covers, which lasted not minutes, not hours, but weeks on end, I found a new stillness. I won't tell you that stillness was gorgeous because it wasn't. It was sticky and foreign and flat. I felt hollowed out, and the more I didn't move, the more nothing else moved around me. There was a darkness to it. It felt like an odd and challenging place I had never intended to visit.

But it was from within that still-stopped-stuckness—that dim and formless place—that everything about the rest of my new pathway began to emanate. In some strange way, stopping like that, unplanned, was the first time in my adult life that I had ever really, *really* let go of what I had been building—trying, succeeding, failing, whatever—long enough to FEEL the stopping, *within me.*

Stopping—real stopping— feels entirely different from slowing down. Real stopping is about not knowing.

Most of us will choose the known over the unknown, even if the known is not that great. Most of us will choose a hard cling to the Logistical Level, with all of its predictable, if sometimes disappointing, certainties, over the subtle, mysterious vibrations of the Essence Level. Most of us resist the stillness and strangeness of the Essence Level's entry point, which is, almost always, stopping. Shifting anything begins, to some degree, with a real STOP.

My life changed because my life stopped. Change came to me—deep, abiding, joyful change. In the aftermath of my having truly come to a halt, an opening was created, because that's what stopping does. It creates the kind of *opening* that rushing forward rarely can.

LEARNING TO STOP

I have often pondered the question of whether *choosing* to stop versus *stopping because life forces you to stop* has any bearing on the beauty of what can come forward as a result.

Do large-scale changes have to be initiated by a kind of "cosmic slap-down" from the Universe? Are there ways to invite and cultivate changes from the inside out? With gentleness? With grace? Is there a way to move beyond the awkward bumbling and emotional car wrecks of navigation-dictated-by-circumstance?

The answer, I have come to believe, is a resounding YES.

In fact, I believe it is ultimately much *better* to step up to the plate and invite the kind of changes you might historically have shied away from if the Universe hadn't "forced" them upon you.

I have made it my mission here to show you how to leverage a newfound desire to stop deeply and to let change flow outward from that stopping, in ways that feel good.

Sometimes I honestly think that either we choose to insert stops and pauses along the way, or they will come and inflict themselves upon us— in forms that are messy and uninvited—upending things that we love. *Choosing* growth and *creating and inviting* the kind of changes we most deeply long for are among the greatest options bestowed upon us as human beings. And it really is an option. Always. Even when it appears, while you tightly cling to the Logistical Level, not to be.

In other words, we can learn to stop. Doing so, in my opinion, is the beginning of everything truer and better.

We can learn to insert stopping into the most difficult *and* the most amazing moments in our lives, and benefit astonishingly from both. The first step is simply reading a chapter like this and considering the possibility that a part of you is hungry to stop.

The second step is beginning to *play* with stopping. At the end of Section 1, you will find a simple SHIFT exercise to try, and I encourage you to do so. But the truth is, you don't even need an exercise. You need only to believe that stopping has value, and to start to experiment with it, even just right this moment. Set down the book. Close your eyes. Breathe. Feel the motion within you. And lean in, with your breathing, to a deep and powerful *inner stopping*, outside of anything and everything, *just right now.*

*　*　*　*　*

See how good that feels? Choosing to stop, and learning to do it well, doesn't guarantee that overwhelming, path-arresting tragedies won't still befall you. But it does open the door to a new way of being, where you are more at the helm or, as I like to say, more "at agency" in your own life.

For me, that dead-stop halt in my thirtieth year was, as it turned out, not just a divorce from a person, but a divorce from an entire way of being, way of navigating, and way of understanding the energies within and around me. I had constructed my world, and my interactions and partnerships within it, from a place based more on fear, scarcity, quick decisions, and movement, and less on a sense of feeling deeply connected to myself, to the Universe, or to much of anything other than the riveting but ill-fated alliance that had presented itself.

Because here's the thing: In that time of transition, when everything came to a complete standstill, everything broken and fallen apart—when I could see only the ending I had so dreaded, with nothing out beyond it—everything clearly and truly done and no longer moving, the strangest thing began to occur.

Little whiffs of a new kind of freedom, clean, light, and whimsical, started popping up, a little at first, and then more and more, all around me.

They felt like strange little synergies—fleeting but real moments of sweetness, synchronicity, and breathing room. Beauty in unexpected places.

These little whiffs did not seem to be coming at me from the Logistical Level at all. Rather, they seemed to be popping up from out of "nowhere." Or, perhaps more specifically, they seemed to be rising up before me—suddenly somehow more visible to me—directly from what I now understand to be the Essence Level.

Strange and increasingly gorgeous coincidences began to happen. Little serendipities and deep-feeling moments began to play out around me. And the more I leaned into them, the more of them there were.

Chapter 5

Essence Coming Alive Within Us

In those strange days at my parents' house, it was almost as if the more broken down and cracked open I became, and the more vulnerable I felt, the more *strange and glorious experiences* I began to discover, popping up around me, delighting and engaging me from increasingly incalculable angles. These odd bits of wonder eventually led the trail to some exhilarating high points, right smack-dab in the center of all that pain, confusion, agony, and uncertainty.

> Everywhere we go, there are
> subtle energetic trails,
> leading beyond Logistics
> to the expansive fluidity of Essence.

After holding steady in that thick, strange stillness for many *long* weeks at my parents' house, I decided to start paying attention to a strange, buzzing sound way in the back of my head. At first, it just came to me as a feeling of agitation, or unease. But as I stayed with it and started to give it a little breathing room, it became more specific. It was more a feeling than words, but if forced to translate it, its wavelength *seemed* to circle around one singular directive:

Head out.

As I leaned into this notion, it fleshed itself out further.

Head out. Any direction is fine. Just get in the car. Pack a few maps. Try not to use them.

This voice, I have come to believe, is not just in me. It is in YOU. Behind your own agitation is very likely some wisdom pushing to get out. You can learn to recognize it. Perhaps my story will help you start doing just exactly that.

I gassed up my car. I scrounged up some maps, a bag of clothes, some car music. A credit card. At a local resale shop, I bought a little three-inch-long figurine: an African black frog artifact that caught my eye, all angles and wiggly white lines.

That one.

I looked him in the eye and he looked right back at me. I felt a shiver within myself. I settled him on the dashboard and pointed the nose of my car and the nose of my new traveling companion toward the sun.

West is good.

I said a wobbly but courageous set of goodbyes to my lovely, bewildered parents, and then I started to drive.

Is it strange that I drove for three months, this way and that, with a tiny black frog as my hitchhiking sidekick? Is it odd that I named him "Savior," and that he felt, to me, like the first safe creature to entrust with the new thoughts that began slowly, gently trickling forth from within me? Yep. I'm pretty sure this is strange. But familiar had been getting me nowhere, and the uncharted and the unknown were calling to me. As I heard myself speak out loud, things were starting to feel ever-so-slightly better, bit by bit. I had not yet learned to communicate directly with myself, but I had some things to say, it turned out, to Savior.

"I have good intuition, Savior," I would opine. "I know I do. But somewhere along the line, I seem to have *stopped using it.* I want it back. I want to hear it."

And then there I would sit, at a stoplight in some small town in Indiana, or Kansas, or Oklahoma, watching the red light click over to green, still and waiting. Waiting … for that tiny little shiver within me that would tell me:

Left, this time.

Or: *Right. Take a right.*

Or: *Straight. Straight on from here. Keep going. Keep going.*

Savior sat silent on the dashboard, perched and ready. Cars behind me would sometimes honk their annoyance. "It's green!" they'd yell through their open windows.

But there I would sit, stopped, waiting for some kind of a feeling. And then at even the smallest inkling of a *hint* of certainty, I would honor the static-filled little awareness that rose up, and make the left. And in that moment, that forward movement, arrived at only by my most concerted attunement to whatever place inside was trying to help me out, I began to feel something like an inner softening—a bud with the promise of an eventual bloom.

What would unfurl before me, as a result of the left turn, or the right, or the straight was, inevitably, something eye-opening. Something beautiful lining the road. Bright blue swaying wildflowers by the thousands that would leave me inhaling more fully. Or widely spaced handmade signs, one after another, triumphantly proclaiming, "I" "LOVE" "YOU" "KEVIN," that would invite me to break the long car-silence with a sudden and unexpected laugh of delight.

Sometimes I would find a brand-new open landscape just *appearing* on the far side of some small town: prairie, or farmland, wide and flat and rolling out golden and open like a brilliant banner, waving its way into the distance, calling to me to breathe deeper and to trust that what I was navigating toward was someplace more true.

I let myself open, increasingly, to this strange new voice, through all the static that, in any other situation, would have played within me as doubt or guilt or background noise. I drove on. I cocked my inner ear to hear it. I deepened the opening within me that might allow me to trust it.

I decided to believe that what I was doing mattered. That there just might possibly be *nothing* that I could be doing of greater value than simply tuning in and aligning with this newly accessed voice. I wanted to discover what would happen if I let this spontaneous, bubbling energy *play out*.

This voice, a whisper of something from deep inside of me at a level of depth I had never before learned to hear, sent me to some unexpected places indeed.

I would be walking on the sidewalk of a small town. *That person*, the voice would seem to say. *Turn around and talk to her.*

Maybe I *had* heard this voice before. Maybe you hear it, too, but become so accustomed to ignoring it you lose track of whatever you once knew of its resonance. It's the second glance we give someone on a bus. It's that fleeting feeling in a crowd: *Do I know her? Should I reach out?*

But we don't.

For those three months, I did.

Me, walking up to a gritty, unshaven man sitting on top of a picnic table somewhere in Wisconsin in a city park: "I am so sorry to bother you. I just have this feeling that—I don't know. There's something I'm trying to figure out, and it seems like you might have part of the answer. Do you have five minutes? Can I tell you what I know, and see if you have something to add to it?"

I was tapping into some strange kind of courage, some irrefutable rising inner momentum. And I was using it to step right into someone's existence. I was asking to be seen, asking others to open toward me, if even just for a moment. Sometimes people assumed I was trying to sell them a Bible or corral them into taking a marketing poll. But most of the time, to my delight, people, when I asked them for input, just piped out variations of, "Okay, sure. What's on your mind?"

"I don't know. I'm hurting, I guess," I would say, to the woman in the parking lot, or to the hotel clerk, or the old man waiting outside the hot dog stand. "I think I was making too many choices based on what I thought looked right. I had this big corporate job, then I owned this big furniture store. I had this big marriage. Now I don't have anything. It feels kind of worse, on the surface. But it feels kind of better, somewhere deeper down. I can't quite make sense of it."

"Do the thing that feels good," the pet shop worker, on break, would tell me.

And it would hit me that this was just *exactly* what I was ready to hear. Precisely. That this was wise. And wonderful. And what I had not been doing, for a long time.

"*Stop saying yes when what you mean is no.*" This from the smiling woman on the elevator, pushing an empty stroller, with a baby on her arm and two little ones poking at each other through her legs.

And when she said it, I heard it deep within me. *Do I say yes to things that don't feel right, deep inside? In what ways do I do that? Is it possible to speak out on one level, and feel legit about it, and yet deny some deeper level within myself that needs to be heard? Is that what I have been doing?* The elevator doors would close in my face, and she would be gone. And there I would be, left holding the thought she had tossed off so easily, feeling it reverberate all through me.

"*Love is a hurtin' thing,*" was what the guy on the picnic table had said. And it felt like a validation of all the pain inside of me. One simple sentence, like a giant key, unlocking something important that I had been holding frozen. Suddenly I was free to simply feel the hurt that I was feeling. No need for fanfare, or even tears. I felt something relax inside of me a little. And the truth of my hurting began to shrink, just a bit. There was one small new space inside me now, opening to the next undiscovered thing.

"*You got this!*" the guy in the tollbooth said. He was only talking about my getting my coin into the white plastic toll bucket, but right then, Essence Level all aglow inside me, *I knew what he meant.* He was talking about *all of it*—rebuilding a life, from the tiny new starting threads up. "You got this," he had said, and I knew, somehow, suddenly, that that was true. I was capable of doing what I barely knew how to define or explain to anyone, including myself. And he was cheering me on.

I was beginning to hear the deeper, more Essence-level reverberations of messages everywhere. Each one felt tailor-made for me, for exactly what I was ready to hear, right then. The student was ready, and the teachers appeared all around—in the flowers, in the wind, in the faces and glances all along the highways and gas stations and tollbooths and back roads of state after state. And I was hungry for their ready wisdom.

"I've been feeling kinda stuck. What do you do when you're stuck?" I would ask, of anyone whose presence gave me that little shiver feeling.

And they would answer me.

I was being spoon-fed my budding new worldview, one appearing-and-disappearing teacher at a time, regardless of whether I had rolled out my whole long tale of woe for them or was just asking for a quick word of wisdom from out of the blue.

The more I did this, the easier the knowing—*whom to ask, how to hear the answer, how to let it grow and build inside of me*—rolled through me and began to take root.

Turn left at the hospital.

Talk to the guy by the pickup truck.

Keep going till you get to Barstow.

They weren't "instructions," really. They were a *knowing* of some sort. An awareness that some important evolution, larger than I was, felt more possible, over here, talking to *this* person or turning in *this* direction, instead of *that* one.

These bite-sized revelations gave way to larger and larger wonderments. Eventually they stopped feeling like random and stand-alone coincidences and conversations. The more I went into stillness, attunement, and trusting, the more I began to feel that the conversation I was in was one gigantic, extended connection. A conversation with everyone: with the Universe itself, with the many places within me that needed some unified way of feeling and seeing the world. It was less about what job I "should" take or whom I "should" align myself with, and more about … well, it wasn't clear yet. But it had something to do with curiosity. And releasing expectations. Not worrying so much what everything "looked" like. And trusting this newly emerging voice within me that seemed to be inviting me to steer my ship in unexpected and eye-opening ways.

I was beginning to understand something: that my focus, my awareness, my attention, was powerful. That whatever I chose to put my energy and attention on would expand.

The more attention you give to that which feels fresh, open, and transporting, the more *transported* you allow yourself to become.

As I watched my life unfold in unforeseen and unimaginable ways, I began to understand something else. The more I opened to the fresh and the new, the more I attracted experiences that were cleansing, healing, and clarifying.

And then something really powerful happened, this time as I wended my way into Nevada.

GENERATING HEALING EXPERIENCES

Now it's June and I am deep into my wandering travels. I am squinting from the brightness. In addition to my silent frog companion, I have been joined by a real-live passenger, Maureen, who is busting out of old patterns herself and has hitched a ride with me to go visit her son in Sacramento. Her company is deeply welcome and we are rolling along coughing up our hard luck tales, doing our level best to tell them without the victim-y undertones we are coming to know have been holding us back.

We are re-inventing ourselves and becoming braver in one another's presence, hopping out of the car to go climb over a barbed-wire fence, to picnic on lunches from grocery store purchases. At a 1950s-looking gas station out in the middle of nowhere, I bow to my inner nine-year-old and buy myself a candy bar while Maureen smokes a cigarette under a bright blue sky so gigantic it swallows the smoke like it never happened. She is not judging my odd, internal navigation system one bit, and I couldn't care less that she is smoking out here in the wide open skies. We're in cahoots, and being with her feels like a gift that I just keep unwrapping.

And that is why, as we are driving 85 miles an hour down the self-proclaimed "Loneliest Road in America" one heat-fest of an afternoon, she doesn't seem in the least bit bothered when I pull over to the side of the road in a sudden dusty halt and grind my car into reverse. Something has caught my eye: some kind of a bandana, tied to an old dusty post, a third of a mile back. I had blown past it, but it had hooked itself into me, poking at my consciousness. The old me would have shaken off the feeling and kept on driving. But by now, *I knew better.*

Backing up full of swerves (who on this planet is truly good at reverse?), I located the post and the dusty bandana wrapped around it. It was next to a nearly invisible dirt driveway—rocks and potholes all over it—that stretched off into the distance. And far, far, *far* away, miles beyond, out there in the middle of the desert, was something very strange indeed. We squinted: Birds, it seemed, were flying up and down, left and right, all in one concentrated area.

I turned the nose of the car down this winding driveway, caution to the wind. Was it five minutes that we were on that odd, twisting trail? Ten? I know only that it was far, and that, newly attuned to a deep kind of clarity rising up within me, *I felt pulled forward.* Maureen was amiably down for whatever. The closer we got, the more of these birds we could see.

Eventually, though, we got close enough to discover that they were not birds at all. They were vehicles. Closer still, we could see, as we pulled into a strange broken-down, tumble-weeded parking lot, they were two-man cars. This long-forgotten lot was filled (*filled!*) with cars linked to trailers housing any number of dune buggies. We were a million miles from anywhere and so wildly off the beaten path that it felt like we no longer really had our bearings at all.

"Are these handmade?" I asked the first person we came to in the parking lot. But he spoke only German (*what?!?!*). The next person was speaking Italian. (*W-h-a-a-a-a-t?*) He pieced together a heavily accented explanation I could only barely decipher before he pointed to another man, curly hair snaking out of his baseball cap, who seemed to be American.

This was in the days before the Internet, so goodness only knows what this really was or how it had all been coordinated, but soon we learned that people from all over the planet had gathered here on this day to ride handmade dune buggies straight up what looked like one of the pyramids of Egypt made entirely of sand. How this impossibly high sand mountain had ended up in the middle of a flat desert I could not fathom.

My cap-wearing new friend invited me for a ride. I had come this far, so I continued on, letting him strap me into the seat and explain to me what a roll-bar was, how we might need it if we ended up turning upside down, and how critical it was that I keep my mouth shut rather than open to avoid sand flying in and suffocating me in the process of riding up over the dune.

Okay.

And then there we were, just me and this stranger, leaving Maureen down there waving supportively on the cracked and weedy asphalt. He revved his engine with pleasure and pride, and then vaulted us up, up, up, UP to the top of that ridiculously high sand peak. I distinctly remember him telling me it was a mile high. Looking back, I can hardly believe such a thing could have been true, but it unquestionably felt like it was.

And there, from that astonishing vantage point, was a view I could never have foreseen or imagined.

There were dozens of them—*dozens* of hills every bit as high, stretched out for *miles* beyond, obscured from the view in the parking lot by this one giant mountain, but clearly visible to me now. Every one of these hills was covered with the same high-flying "birds"—dozens and dozens of dune buggies of all shapes and sizes, all of them filled with scruffy-looking male drivers in crash helmets. The buzz of them filled the air like bees. And yet before I had another moment to take all of this in, my snake-haired friend shot our vehicle down the back side of that sand mountain at *a zillion miles an hour.*

The bottom of my stomach dropped out. I felt myself curl and tuck inward at the sheer speed and drop of it. It felt almost like more than I could manage.

And then, halfway down ... from deep, deep, *d-e-e-e-p* in my being ... I started to laugh.

I laughed like I had never laughed before. I laughed from a place within me I did not know existed—wide and open and joyful and free of pain, confusion, or disappointment. I laughed with my mouth wide open—for a split second, before I remembered the caution he had given me about the sand flying in. I laughed in a way that moved all through me, tears flying off of my face, and left disintegrating behind us in our wake. Down we went, up we went, down we went, up we went, and all the while I felt more exhilarated than I could ever remember feeling.

Months of hurt and smallness, miscalculation and desperation rippled up and flew off of me in *waves*, one after another as we dipped and ascended each gigantic sand mound. All of life was a series of drops and ascensions, wind and sand, and an endless big wild blue sky under a sparkling, radiating sun. The heat, the shivers, the thrill, the wonder, the uncertainty, the security of it—all of it struck me as an exact replica of everything good I had ever known about prior to this moment. I cannot say whether we were up there for two minutes or for twenty.

I felt untethered entirely from the details of my life and deeply *present and belonging* in this moment of Pure Essence. I could feel years passing through me, clarifying and revising themselves into something larger that served my forward movement more clearly: powerful journeys, blazing truths, releases on a scale close to eternal. How many dozens of therapy sessions might it have taken to achieve such a clearing within me? Who can say, and what does it matter?! Something powerful and cleansing was happening! I was alive, and I was free—free from the drama, the stories I had written about how unlovable I had become, how unsalvageable things were, how unfortunate the situation was, how long I might have to hurt, how disconnected I surely must have allowed myself to become. All of that seemed tiny and unnecessary, remote and extraneous. I was fully alive and awake in that very moment.

Eventually, the driver brought the dune buggy back down to the scraggly parking lot where he offered Maureen a journey of her own. I sat there joyfully panting while the two of them rode off to a pinpoint and then returned triumphant.

How do you thank someone for a freely offered gift that *changes everything?* I wobbled onto my feet and put forth whatever words of gratitude I could think of. Then I turned, with Maureen, back to my car—the same person I had been before we arrived but also someone entirely ablaze and alive, filled with hope and possibility, freedom, and the bone-deep joy of release and rediscovery.

Whatever strangeness you want to attach to this story—to noticing a bandana in the middle of nowhere, backing up, turning toward the unknown for pothole-riddled miles, and then discovering the oddest of secret treasures (one that could heal hurt places inside through the sheer unexpected wonder of flying forward nose-first into the unknown)—one thing is sure. In a season full of clinging to the shrinking remains of the end of the line, full of dead ends and shutdowns, I had started sniffing out a new pathway. And the more I tuned in to it, the more I found it. The more I stopped, the more available it became. The more I honored it, the more the stillness brought yet another opening, another step, another whiff, another clue. And the more I trusted what I was hearing, the more the world rose up to meet me exactly, unpredictably, healingly, right where I needed it most.

I love sharing this story because it is a reminder to me that daring to make choices based on re-connecting with those odd, "knowing" inner voices can be a powerful thing indeed. But I also think of it as my first "smack-me-over-the-head-with-it" experience of how, underneath everything, at every moment, just beneath the surface of all the pain and small stories we carry around, is a huge, healing, present, available, expansive world filled with the energy of YES.

DARING TO SEE AND INVITE SOMETHING FINER

All the time, right within reach, is the Essence Level of reality, where life is ripe with possibility, where the unexpected holds the wonder, where there is breathing room and a timeless amount of time to FEEL and TRY and LEARN and eventually to LAUGH, dammit! To laugh at the way it all seemed so hard and stuck when, really, the only thing keeping me stuck was my fear of letting go of feeling stuck! Of thinking I could keep everything just how it had been, yet somehow keep growing. Of holding tight and clamping down when all of life is such a powerful invitation to stop clinging to outdated "certainty" and to start wondering.

There is not a scenario in the world that would have occurred to me while driving down the Loneliest Road in America that would have had me believing I was a few short minutes away from a kind of healing that would remain unparalleled in my lifetime. Unparalleled for its intensity and through-sweeping ability to wash out months—years—of pain, and to rather definitively "re-boot" me, as it did, onto a path of living forward with enthusiasm and a giant, playful question mark about what's next. Always, below everything, there exists a constant, streaming energy of possibility and larger context. It is not hiding from us, but we have to learn to look.

The road to our answers is in us.

The pathway to that better place is glistening around you, and within you, even now. Not just me, but *you*.

My answers started coming not because my hand was forced by the loss of my home or by my divorce. Not really. My answers started coming because I decided I wanted to hear my own inner voice; I wanted to locate my own internal answers. I decided daring to learn how to do that was worth my time and attention. I decided to be a novice, to start back at the beginning, to be willing to be not good at it, but to lean into it anyway. To set out and see if I could find what was in the air all around me, what was right under my nose, and what was rumbling, deep within me.

You do not need to wonder whether your answers will come to you or not. If you stop for real and tune in with a genuine hunger to know, you will find your answers—your pathway to something truer, something finer, something deeper—within and around you. Not necessarily instantaneously. Not gift-wrapped in perfect shiny paper with everything all solved so all you need to do is sit back and enjoy the finished product. It doesn't seem to work exactly like that. But I have come to believe this with a certainty that feels validated everywhere I turn, in my life-coaching work, in my music-making, and in my very own life: *Your answers are inside you.* You can start to tune into them. Right now. There is nothing, actually, to wait for. You can begin this in a way that invites you to wake up and meet your very own self and your very own life, on your very own *growing edge.*

I have seen it too many hundreds of times in too many hundreds of situations and settings now, and I want to help you experience this yourself.

In the moment that we choose with full intention to tune in and really hear from the Essence Level within and around us, powerful shifts begin to come forward, for each of us, without exception: Clarity. A newfound sense of certainty. Vibrancy. A feeling of readiness. A sense of purpose. A sense of wonder. An inner generosity and confidence. A feeling of relief. A new kind of exhilaration. A whole new wavelength of authenticity.

And bubbling forward, at a newly sustainable level:

JOY.

Chapter 6

YES Right Now: Takeaways & Explorations

I'd like to bring us into completion on Section 1, Shift the Balance, by sharing some key takeaways and offering a SHIFT exercise you can try on your own. It represents one way (though there are an infinite number of "ways in") that you can start playing with reorienting (from being purely Logistically Focused to a more Essence- *and* Logistics-Oriented state of being).

Everything in this summarizing chapter is designed to help you do one thing, really: to discover for yourself that it is possible to exist on two levels of reality at once. In fact, it's not only do-able (the more you explore this, the more you will see it's true), but life also *feels so much better* when you do.

You were *built* for the Logistical Level. There is so much you can do in this world, to lean into and to master setting clear goals, establishing meaningful deadlines and boundaries, and to learn to anticipate and sculpt the likely outcomes.

But you were *born* for the Essence Level. You were born for living fully into the wonders of serendipity, coincidence, beauty, depth, and love.

In short, I want to help you grab the reins on not just one but both levels, and to *feel something bigger* as you do so. This will tee us up nicely for the second part of our journey, in Section 2: learning how to not only overcome the dramas that hold you back, but also to use them as fuel for deepening your connection with yourself.

So let's review.

KEY TAKEAWAYS OF SECTION 1

1. **TWO REALITIES** – The realm of "being" that most of us are oriented toward is very Logistically based (clocks, calendars, deadlines, scientific principles, and the predictable rise and fall of emotion and drama). But there is a second realm of reality playing out, simultaneously, all the time (wonder, possibility, beauty, great leaps of insight, coincidences, intuition, powerful shifts of energy). That's the Essence Level, and when you are regularly, consciously tapped into not *just* the Logistical Level but the Essence Level *as well,* your experience becomes much more vibrant, connected, and alive.

2. **STUCKNESS AND FLOW** – On the Essence Level, energy FLOWS, expansively and serendipitously—ripe with possibility in an ongoing, otherworldly kind of way. On the Logistical Level, flow and stuckness vacillate. Sometimes doors open and things can really move. Other times things become stuck, sludgy, overwhelming, or even catastrophically shutdown. The more the Essence Level becomes a part of your experience, the more the energy in your life tends toward flow.

3. **VOICES WITHIN** – There is a second, stronger, albeit softer, voice within each of us that is already deeply connected to the Essence Level. This voice has a distinct vibration which is filled with possibility, options, clarity, and flow. The place within us from which this voice comes grasps a larger picture and, from that vantage point, can make unique connections and observations. Waking up to the presence of this voice and this place within us can make a powerful difference in our lives. (We will talk much more about this in Section 3.)

4. **STOPPING** – We limit ourselves in thinking that Essence moments only "appear"—pop into and then pop back out of our lives—in rare, brief spurts that are beyond our grasp. In fact, we can learn to orient ourselves toward the Essence Level and intentionally *invite in* much more of that flowing, serendipitous energy. We do this by *stopping*—ceasing to feed a connection to reality that is purely Logistically based. When we do so, we can begin to hear this new voice rising within us.

5. **ESSENCE WITHIN YOU** – Once you have stopped, it becomes far more possible for you to sense the Essence Level all around you,

and, in so doing, to begin to attune to a similar kind of energy within yourself. From this point of awareness, so much more is possible!

* * * * *

TRY THIS: THE ESSENCE SHIFT

You will discover three SHIFTS in this book: The Essence Shift, the Pivot Shift, and the Pulse Shift. Before I lay out the first one for you, I'd like to share some thoughts about the dynamics of SHIFTS in general.

A SHIFT, as I am defining it here, is any small internal movement that makes a big difference. It's a conscious energetic alteration that you invite and allow *inside of you.* When a SHIFT happens within, the energy *outside* of you, all around you, moves and changes in response. The more you take the time to SHIFT, the more flowing and supportive the energy around you tends to become.

Engaging in a SHIFT any time—when you have some spare time, when you feel desperate or overwhelmed, or as a regular practice that just feels good—invites flow. It's a way to be purposeful about creating a conscious opening in yourself significant *enough* to return you to a more rightful, flowing, ease-filled state of being.

> You determine what gets stuck within you
> and what flows easily based entirely on
> your willingness to create
> a space within yourself
> where energies can SHIFT.

When you practice SHIFTS, tiny little magical things tend to happen. The more you practice them, the more magical things tend to happen. This is not so much because SHIFTS are magical in their own right, but because when you begin seeing this moment—any moment—as an opportunity to expand yourself and grow (and when you approach this with *intentionality* and a little support), you literally change the energetic dynamics of what has gotten stuck, repetitive and small, inside you. You *free yourself up* in a new way—even if just for a moment. When you are freed up, new avenues can open within you to allow *more direct alignment with the larger energies all around you.*

THE ESSENCE SHIFT

This little repeatable practice is built on the simple idea that access to the Essence Level is always just one conscious SHIFT away from where you are now. It's about remaining grounded in the Logistical World you know and love (most of the time), but instead of staying entirely focused there, gently *tipping the balance of your consciousness* more toward Essence. It's like shifting the focus of your "weight" from an emphasis on Logistics to an increased emphasis on Essence.

CONCEIVE OF ESSENCE   DIP YOUR TOE IN   SHIFT THE BALANCE

When the balance tips, with *more* of your awareness and emphasis residing on the Essence Level (even as you still exist and move about on the Logistical Level in your everyday life), the wonders of the authentic world deep within you and the wonders of the powerful, gorgeous Essence energies all around you can begin to dance and come alive in new ways. It is this kind of energetic playfulness that translates directly into a deeper resonance and happiness—into a Deeper YES.

THE ESSENCE SHIFT:
FIVE STEPS FOR SHIFTING THE BALANCE

Try this SHIFT whenever you feel neutral or good,
and like the idea of feeling *more*.

1. **Stop** – Take several deep, centering breaths with your eyes closed. Invite your connection to the Logistical Level to come into stillness as you breathe, making room for something different, something unknown, something more.

2. **I Am Ready** – State aloud an authentic, original-to-you expression of wanting to invite more Essence energy into your consciousness, generally, and into this moment right now, specifically. Invite an experience that is significant enough to be felt but not large enough to overwhelm. With this in mind, state aloud, "I am ready to sense and feel Essence."

3. **I Am Open** – Open yourself up to any form of help that is available to you—from deep within, from energies all around you, from your god, from powerful beings living or dead, from a sense of luck and possibility, from angels, heroes, the fates, or any other positive force. State aloud, "I am open to loving assistance."

4. **Constrict** – Inhale deeply, then tighten or clench all of your muscles, holding the clench for the count of ten. Focus especially on the tightness of your fists, arms, closed eyes, and jaw muscles, biting down hard. Try swiftly rubbing the curled fingers of one clenched fist against the lower palm of the other hand, creating a friction, a heat, and an awareness of this constricted, pinched energy.

5. **Invite a Shift** – Now slowly exhale, inviting an energetic shift within you of any size, in any form that is authentic—a shiver, a new knowing, a release, a calming, a feeling of lightness, a sense of invigoration, an image coming to mind, etc. Continue breathing into this SHIFT until it feels complete. Look around you. Stay alert for a sense of expansiveness, ease, wonder, connection, clarity, or joy.

Living the Deeper YES

Variations on this SHIFT include doing it in the presence of a friend, for added energy and "legitimacy;" doing it in a favorite spot in nature; doing multiple repeats on the breathing and clenching portion, as desired; substituting fast nose breathing for constricting; or making a long verbal sound as part of the exhale—choosing one note to sustain as long as possible that most closely matches the "clench" of your body.

WILL THIS SHIFT REALLY MAKE A DIFFERENCE?

Like anything else in life, so *much* of whether this SHIFT helps you or not has to do with where *within yourself* you approach it from.

Can you approach it from an open-hearted, open-minded, hopeful place? I know that can be hard to do, especially if you are feeling down (the SHIFT in Section 2 is specifically for times like that). But in whatever state you decide to try this SHIFT, I invite you to ask yourself, *"Who am I helping, really, when I resist stepping all the way in and giving this exercise* (or ANY exercises or offerings of assistance from anyone I trust, for that matter) *the fullest chance possible?"*

It's possible you are sensing a strong urge to find fault with this offering, to search for proof that your experience of it might be something less than amazing. But does this urge really serve you to the fullest? Or does it shield you—from failure, yes, but also, perhaps, from vulnerability, openness, potential, and success?

What if your resistant orientation, if you have one, is simply a form of fear? And what if the antidote to that fear is its exact opposite? Fear's opposite, if you ask me, is not so much courage as it is *curiosity.*

What might become possible for you, in playing with this SHIFT, if you allowed skepticism to give way, even for a short time, to curiosity?

The answer lies within you. It lies within this exact moment, in which you decide to try this, or to fight against it. Or to try, but in a "fighting it" way. Or—wonder of wonders—to give in fully, like a dune-buggy rider out in the middle of nowhere, dropping into a feeling that is RIGHT THERE to be felt, as soon as resistance is released, even just for a moment.

The biggest part of this exercise is not how exactly you follow the steps suggested here (Revise them as you see fit! Invite them to work for you!), but rather, it is in the place within yourself from which you step forward now. I invite you to really try this. The big stretch is in how fully you turn yourself over to a sense of possibility—how fully you honor the place within you that *wants* to have the fullest possible experience of trying this ... and so much more.

Be open, willing, curious. Repeatedly. Find out what it is that has brought you this far.

Try it now. There is only this moment.

* * * * *

From here, we are ready to launch you into Section 2. Our journey has begun with hope and potential. But we can't dive fully into the fruits of Section 3—a whole new way of dialoguing with yourself on the inside—until we have dealt with whatever you imagine to be the roadblocks in your life, which is what Section 2 is all about.

I'm talking about looking more closely and discerningly at the stories you tell yourself about what hurts, what holds you back, and why. I want to help you with shifting those stories, with shifting the related "realities," and with your own emancipation from the way those very stories may have shackled you, unnecessarily.

It begins, then, with teaching you how to look squarely at the obstructions and dramas that are holding you back and then to ... *CHANGE YOUR MIND.*

SECTION 2

CHANGE YOUR MIND

YOU AND OTHER PEOPLE

*"It ain't what you don't know that gets you in trouble. It's what you know for sure that **just ain't so.**"*

—Mark Twain

In this section, I intend to show you ...

How you have probably been
giving away huge quantities of
your energy and power
without even realizing you are doing it.

How, in this lower-power state,
you are far more likely to
repeat negative patterns and dramas,
reinforcing stuck places within yourself.

And how you can reclaim this power,
reduce the upsets in your life,
and learn to see others
and yourself more clearly.

The process for transforming all of this can feel
new, strange, and unfamiliar,
because it involves

CHANGING YOUR MIND
about what is happening to you,
how bad, or *not* bad, it is,
and about how much (vs. how little) inner power
you actually have.

Chapter 7

When Things Are Going Badly

Sometimes things suck.

Days that feel promising at the outset can get pretty derailed, and they often do. Worse still, some days—too many of them—can look bad right from the start. Waking up with a sense of dread or a low-boiling stomach clench is a good sign that *"suck-age,"* in all its glory, is already going on.

There is, we tell each other, so much that is out of our control.

If *we* were running the show, things would be different. We would not run it like this. If only *he* would handle this more communicatively; if only *she* did not keep poking her nose into the middle of everything, *we* would be fine. And we believe it.

So this is where a lot of us live, a lot of the time: in a world where the power belongs to someone else, where we find ourselves running around trying to head the worst of it off at the pass, or where we are working hard to respond instantaneously so we can get things back on track. Or, maybe more often than feels good, where we are accepting how crummy things are, and then feeling bitter or righteous or depressed or just generally zapped as a result.

And that means we are operating from a deficit.

But what if we turned the tables, and instead of digging out of a hole, we built on the ideas from Section 1 and started *feeling more amazing now,* by tuning into the Essence Level more consciously, rather than *waiting* for Logistical events to conspire around us to "give us permission" to feel better? This is something of a radical concept, and it's what Section 2 is really about.

What if our outlook wasn't so much, *When things go better around here, then I can feel amazing*, but rather *I can feel amazing any time I am ready to, and the rest will follow.*

<blockquote>

When we make ourselves ripe to tap in and feel more alive, events around us begin to conform to that aliveness.

</blockquote>

What if the upsets of others no longer triggered you? And the dramas unfolding around you started to appear to you not as reasons to get bent out of shape, but rather as *voices calling you deeper*—like doors opening, one after another, inviting you into a place within yourself where you were more clear, more powerful, less reactive, and more able to PLAY with the intense energy coming at you, rather than get knocked edgewise by it?

This is not possible when you are caught up in the strong, tantalizing pull of drama (he said, she said, he should, she should) in your own life, because drama has an uncanny way of *obscuring the real issues*.

But there are ways of moving out beyond the little dramas of our lives that can help us have much easier and more regular access to the Essence Level.

I believe that time can "expand" or "shrink" with the focus of your consciousness. And I have come to believe that the more you understand about not just the flow of time in the conventional sense, but the flow of what I like to call "Ceremonial Time," on the Essence Level, the more you can access your own power, way out beyond the dips and curves of the little dramas all around you.

AN INTRODUCTION TO CEREMONIAL TIME

It is 7:15 on a Saturday morning and I am a high school junior, sitting in the passenger seat beside my friend Rick. It's an unusually icy morning, and he and I are on our way into the city to do a re-take on our SAT tests.

Driving on a divided highway, Rick sees the car ahead of him slowing, so he puts on his brakes too hard and weird things start to happen.

The car does a 180-degree turn, so now we are facing backward on the highway. This is quite an odd feeling. Soon we are spinning farther, shooting across the median and into the fast-moving oncoming traffic of the opposite highway lanes. Neither of us is speaking, and everything is happening fast, and slow; blurred, yet also, simultaneously, somehow wildly clear. I am experiencing a strange pacing of time I am not acquainted with. And yet my mind, strangely relaxed and open, begins easily pondering mathematical calculations on the angles, the speed, the vectors of our trajectory, and the movement of the cars coming at us on the icy opposite lanes.

In real time, this lasts three seconds—maybe five. But inside my mind, free of anything but this exact moment, I have all the breathing room I could possibly need, and I can sense so much more than usual: by the time the cars hurtling toward us align with the spot where we are spinning and twirling, we will be on the other side of the divided highway. And, given the velocity at which we are moving, I somehow seem to just deeply *know* that we will slide not into the oncoming cars, but instead straight into the shallow ditch on the other side of the road.

I note all of this with ease and a certainty that, still to this day, I find fascinating. By the time we reach the ditch, I can see—still in this gorgeous, vivid, strange ballet of speed and cars and sliding tires and ice—the car will have rotated yet another 180 degrees and the level of my head, once we enter the ditch, will be perfectly aligned with the thick, protruding truncated branch of a fast-approaching dead tree.

And so then, it's time to bend, I think to myself, in a voice that feels soothing, loving, wise, and clear. The entire thing feels as simple as a scene choreographed down to the millimeter and rehearsed dozens of times.

And so I bend, utterly un-frightened, clearheaded, and just exactly as flexible as I need to be, in just exactly the instant that such a movement has become an irrefutably necessary choice.

POW! The passenger side window of the car is slammed wide open into a thousand dazzling pieces.

And where my head had been seconds before, there is now this massive, truncated branch, protruding straight into the car. Right where my face was. Right where my brain was. Right where all of the soft tissue of my head was.

But me? I am doubled down beneath it, soft as a rag doll, my face against my toes. The car has come to a rest. The tree branch, thrust right through the glass of the window where my head was, has stopped it. It is frozen there, above the gentle curve of my back.

In the aftermath, I have often turned that moment over in my mind like a comforting, smooth stone in my pocket. On a Logistical Level, one might say it was adrenaline that saved me. But on the Essence Level, I hold an awareness that something else entirely was happening for me that morning.

The moments leading up to the impact of that branch through the window rest magically in my memory as a "grand opening" of Essence-energy in my life. It was my first conscious, extended Essence Level experience. And, relatedly, it was my introduction to Ceremonial Time. In Logistical Time, it really was just a few seconds. On the Essence Level, in Ceremonial Time, it brought about a grand expansion within me that allowed me to drop into a timeless place of ease and possibility.

LEARNING TO RECOGNIZE CEREMONIAL TIME

In Ceremonial Time, your consciousness is alive and awake, but it extends into something wholly other—something deeply *Essence*. It's not about the ticking of seconds on the minute hand of any clock, anywhere. It's a level of attention and awareness (to *certain* aspects of the energy around and within you) and a level of non-engagement, or *non-attachment* (to *other* aspects of it). It's a kind of access to a healthy string of previous experiences and possible future vantage points in your life, shimmering behind you and available to you now, in all their fullness. It's the decision to stop clinging to the "smaller story" and, more and more, to trust that at the heart of every being, including you, and every experience, including the one you are having right now, is expansive, helpful energy, available to come forward and work its way into your consciousness, where it can actualize and be celebrated.

Section 2, then, is all about what it means to be inside of a difficult moment in *a uniquely awake and powerful way.*

A CHALLENGING MOMENT RE-IMAGINED

What if, in Ceremonial Time, there is no such thing as "too late?" What if all there is, is this one singular moment, and it runs deeper and is filled with more options than you might ever have guessed?

What if you, in a centered state, were approached by someone triggered and upset (furious, ranting, blaming, etc.)? What if, despite their upset, you had the inner spaciousness to choose who you wanted to be, how you wanted to be, and what resources within yourself to tap into, so that you could express a version of yourself that you LOVE: wise, big-picture-thinking, attuned, and creative?

What if you could SEE right through *a-a-a-a-l-l* the many layers of toxic energy this other upset person might be caught up in (the drunken bar fight, the delayed airport fight, the tantrum-ing toddler, the angry co-worker) right through to Who They Truly Are—to the wonder of this other being—as you paused whatever was happening inside of you long enough to simply *see more.*

When you know how to shift your conscious gaze and look through a more powerful, penetrating lens at any given moment, you experience more options for *who you can choose to be in the face of that moment:*

> # You are powerful enough to see challenging experiences through the lens of Ceremonial Time and, in so doing, change the course of them.

THE POWER INSIDE ONE INSTANT

Viktor Frankl, celebrated Holocaust survivor, has said, "Between stimulus and response there is a space. In that space is our power to choose our response. In our response lies our growth and our freedom."

The fullness of your power lies in the exact space after something has occurred and before you respond.

On the Logistical Level, that space can seem invisible. But from an Essence perspective, it is always right there. Your choice lies in whether you show up either fully present or reactive, whether you extend a hand as a slap or as a caress; your choice lies in whether you create a message of "YES" in any given moment or a message of "NO." All your power lives in the deep increments of Ceremonial Time that exist *just before you respond.*

Reactivity is the limiting belief that you are unable to access the breathing room you need before you respond.

There are innumerable options as you face any kind of a trigger or upset in yourself or in another, and only a miniscule percentage of them look anything like being reactive, getting upset, lashing out, or turning away.

What if you dared to see more options in any given moment of upset?

You can preserve your inner well-being, access the benevolent powers within you, and use them wisely *any time.* You can pause right now and insert into this very moment the breathing room it takes for you to make loving, moment-expanding, surprising, learning-filled choices. Over time this can become less and less like a focused exertion and more and more like something as simple and natural as an exhale.

THE END OF REACTIVITY

On day one of my graduate school experience at the University of Santa Monica (USM), my teacher Dr. Ron Hulnick stood before a room of more than a hundred of us and said a strange and extraordinary thing he had heard from the spiritual teacher Ram Dass many years before. I wrote it down immediately. I have been working with this idea ever since:

"Growing up, no one ever told me that things could be going badly and I could be doing well."

Section 2 is all about the journey of understanding and living into that sentiment. It's about what it means to be "doing well" simply because I am honoring an inner truth that I am doing well, regardless of what may be going on around me.

Picture a world where your own energy and the energy of others are never confused. Picture a world where situations that would have hurt you now have the power to expand and soften you. Where experiences that might have threatened you now either (a) awaken you on a much deeper level if it serves the highest good or (b) can be recognized as the harmless illusions that they are and melt right out of your consciousness.

Reactivity is the inability to get the breath you need. If we look closer, we can see how frighteningly skillful we are at keeping ourselves wrapped in drama and gasping for breath—not because we don't *want* centeredness or love in our lives, but because we haven't received the internal support we need to learn how to CHANGE OUR MINDS about who we can choose to be, in the moment after stimulus and before response.

What is it that clouds our ability to see? What draws us toward the stickiness of getting lost in the upset? What keeps us from being Who We Most Deeply Are when we are triggered?

The answer lies in the brilliant distraction of drama and our role at the very center of that.

Chapter 8

The Brilliant Distraction of Drama

I think most of us have it backward. We spend a LOT of time and energy sustaining hard, dispiriting hits, disappointments, setbacks, and frustrations because we are more oriented toward what is happening "out there" in the world of interactions with others than is actually optimal for us. And, at *the very same time*, we are significantly less focused on what's happening "in here" (in the inner workings of our own feelings and thoughts and desires and deep needs) than is necessary for the brilliance of our system to run as it is designed to run—with ease and grace.

I can't tell you how many times individuals have come to me with two "separate" issues that they want coaching help with. It often goes something like this:

1. I have this thing that I really *want* to do (this article I want to write, this hobby I want to start, this trip I want to take, this marriage I want to focus on more fully). I am clear that I want this. Can you help me get moving on it? I feel so stuck.

2. Oh, and by the way, can you also help me with this other time-sucking problem (computer games, binge-watching TV, gossip addiction) that I spend way too much time on?

If you're looking at this from the outside, the math on this equation seems almost laughable. *Stop playing computer games and use the time to plan your trip, write your article, or engage in your hobby.*

Done. Next?

Of course, if it were that simple, we wouldn't hire life coaches, or struggle with time management issues at all. We would just wait for traveling mathematicians to walk around and point it out to us when we were using our time in ways that aligned with what we most deeply want, and when we were not.

"Oh, thank you, Mathematician!" we would say. "I had not noticed that the math was off in this equation. I will quickly make a change, stop with the drug use, start up that new landscaping business I have been dreaming of, and all will be well."

It doesn't work like this because there is something *very sticky* about that computer game. Or that drug use. Or *whatever it is* that is happening when, upon reflection, we wish something else had been happening instead.

STICKINESS

I'm talking about stickiness, as in the shiny flypaper contraption my grandmother had dangling from her kitchen ceiling to keep the flies off the food. I don't know that the flies cared that the flypaper was housed in a decorative golden cardboard sheath. But what those flies DID care about was that it was pulsing out a kind of pheromone—*throm, throm, throm*—that was unbelievably alluring to them. So they hauled their little fly-tails over there and landed on the paper to get the best possible whiff of this stuff. And then what was all over the paper? A gluey coating. Their fly-feet stuck to the paper, and good luck getting out of there! Once their feet were caught, the deal was pretty much sealed.

It's not so different for us with the allure of games on the computer or any other distraction like Web surfing, that extra drink, or another handful of chips. They all fall under the category of "things that feel good while I am doing them but that are hard to stop and that keep me from things that would feel good to me on an even deeper, more rewarding level, if I knew how to navigate myself there without getting caught up in *this*."

We get caught up in the stickiness of some little activity that, from the outside, *appears* to be something we can just pop in, do a little of, and then pop back out. "Appears" being the operative word here, because we all have loads of experience to the contrary.

I'll play the game for ten minutes before bed, just to wind down. I had a hard day and there's no harm in ten minutes, we think to ourselves. And then somehow it is 2 a.m. and here we sit, zombie-eyed and gearing up *for just one more round,* even though tomorrow we have a very full schedule and sleep would make more sense.

I'll just knock off a couple of these little items on my to-do list, I tell myself. *And then I'll dive in on the big project I've been dancing around.* Two long hours later, I have, in fact, slayed a bunch of the bite-sized, doable tasks that have been on my list for, admittedly, a naggingly long time. (*This is great! Look how productive I was!*) And yet none of these little items were particularly urgent or important to me, really. They make me feel competent and efficient. I am on solid ground when I am executing them because they are familiar tasks. But the truth is, I am not one millimeter closer to that larger, more meaningful project that I truly do care about and long to engage with. That project represents more of a stretch. That project is calling me forward into something new and unknown that I hunger for but am perhaps a little daunted by. And that project is less of a "safe place to hide," really, from my own potential and growth than the smaller things I chose to do instead.

We get caught in the stickiness because it is alluring. Because it calls to a place within us, *nearer to the surface,* that wants to feel good and can make a pretty decent case, on the fly (pardon the pun), for why it wants to, deserves to, and can handle just a little indulgence and then "get right back to it."

We get caught in the stickiness because it does make us pretty happy, while we are doing it, most of the time. Maybe not big-picture happy. But little-picture happy anyway. Logistical Level happy. And what's so wrong with that? *We can't all be climbing mountains every minute of the day, can we?,* we ask ourselves, pleading our case.

We get caught in the stickiness, finally, because the stickiness is our comfort zone. Because it is a place where we can shut down and avoid the discomfort that might be associated with growing, stretching, stepping into the unknown.

What we miss,
when we get stuck in our comfort zone,
is the opportunity to engage
with someplace deeper, truer, and
more alive within us.

In the battle of "computer games vs. meaningful activity" or "ticking off the easy stuff vs. turning to the more powerful invitations that promise deeper satisfaction," or even "start an argument vs. take a vulnerable next step," we find the very same dynamics that are present in choosing to focus our attention "out there vs. in here." There is a stickiness to the allure of what is playing out "out there" that tempts us to focus heavily outward, often *at the expense of* our ability to tune in to what is calling to us "in here."

The stickiness "out there" is the drama we participate in and help to co-create, over and over again, with such variety and abandon that it can sometimes be hard to even spot the patterns until we slow ourselves down and receive something of a guided tour.

MOVING PAST STICKINESS

I want to share with you what I have learned about connecting more directly, more clearly, and more meaningfully with the most tender and wise places deep within. But I can't, without first helping you to move aside the external drama that so cleverly stands in the way of that, so much of the time.

If a tug "out there" is strong (the "stickiness" of another computer game, another drink, another fight with your kids), then I invite you to consider the possibility that it is strong for a good, healthy, helpful reason.

NOT for reasons you are used to thinking, like:

- because I am weak.
- because I just really need a break.
- because of all the crappy things that have been happening to me "out there" that I need to deal with, in a minute, after one more computer game …

What if the tug "out there" is not actually about "out there" at all? What if the tug is strong for a completely different (and exciting) reason, as it relates to your growth?

> ## When the tug "out there" is strong, it is a signal—a marker— telling you that things inside of you are off balance and in need of your immediate attention.

What if I could show you how the tug you are experiencing—toward numbing activities *and* toward the drama of upsets, altercations, and indignities—has a great value because it is designed to call your attention to *a corresponding dynamic*—something unhealed, unfinished, unattended to—*within yourself*. And what if healing THAT is easier (and more eye-opening and joyful) than you might have guessed? Easier, in the big picture, than getting caught up in petty dramas around you or getting sucked into the numbing space of your own comfort zone, swirling around in the bottom of a drink or at the finish line of another computer game?

DRAMA AS A SOLUTION

Most of us experience drama as something that happens "to" us. We get "hit" by upsetting events and as a "result" we retreat into our comfort zones. But I want to invite you to look deeper, underneath your own stories of upset, to see if we might be able to locate places within you that perhaps *invite* such dramas, and even *co-create* them.

You may not realize you do this, but I think you will find it illuminating and freeing to consider that you are very likely an active participant in the dramas "coming at" you. This is not a bad thing at all, as long as you learn to see your tugs toward drama (or numbing out) as a simple flag, waving in front of you, saying, "It's time to turn inward!"

We've all heard stories of people who struggle and struggle to break an addiction to cigarettes, with no lasting success. And others who, one day, see the situation from a different angle and then simply never touch another cigarette again.

I want to help you see your situation from a different angle. I want to invite you to consider that drama, upset, and numbness are not bad. They are the exact points where you can locate the power needed to transform your perspective and CHANGE YOUR MIND about what is really happening and who you are capable of being in the face of it. Drama, when it appears to rise up before you, is the place where you <u>get to</u> make powerful choices about Who You Really Are.

Drama is the growing edge of your ability to deepen your relationship with yourself.

Who we are, in the moment that drama flashes up around us, has everything to do with whether we choose to <u>turn away from</u> our deeper self OR to <u>turn toward</u> our deeper self, in the instant when we need ourselves the most. But I'm here to tell you that although turning against others in a moment of drama may appear to save us from turning against ourselves, aiming upset outward, when viewed through the lens of the Essence Level, is one of the most potent forms of self-savagery. It may be a well-disguised form, but it is fiercely damaging nonetheless.

We are not quite ready for all of that yet, but we are getting closer.

We are entering into the land of seeing through new eyes how we all participate (whether we know it or not) in stirring up and fanning the flames of drama, whipping them into a grand distraction of epic proportions.

We are entering into a place where you might begin to ask yourself,

How much distraction power have I given over to external drama?

Upon closer inspection, this whole "giving away power to drama" thing is not as complex as it first seems. I promise. Everything that drama kicks up comes down to one little thing: what I like to call energetic "charge." So let's look at what energetic charge is, how it gets activated, and what powerful options we have when it does.

Chapter 9

Upsets and Charge

I am sitting in my Master's program at USM. I am thirty years old, and I am learning something that surely can't be right. It sounds like such an impossible idea. And yet somehow, it strikes me as an awareness I have always *sort of* had.

In class I am learning that whether what I am experiencing is fear, or anger, or incapacitation—whether I am cringing, cowering, attacking, or stuck frozen in place by my own judgments against myself or others—ALL of this, really, is just one thing, energetically.

Every upset you ever experience is simply an energetic charge.

An upset—*any* upset that I experience—means that there is a current of disturbance running through me. Somehow, something uncomfortable and unsettled has been activated within me, crackling, popping, and jolting me in some manner.

CHARGE AS A WAKE-UP CALL

As I sit there in class, it is slowly beginning to dawn on me that, on some deep and fundamental level, perhaps all of the upsets I have ever had really <u>are</u> all the same thing. They look different; they carry with them different narratives and explanations that I can easily get caught up in. And because I *can* get easily caught up in those differences, I have been missing the real opportunity. When I am upset, there is a charge running through me, and it is that charge—that feeling—that *can*, if I let it, be a wake-up call to go deeper and find out what is happening inside.

It starts occurring to me that, just possibly, my desire to see all of the upsets in my life in terms of how they are different—how unrelated they all appear because of the stories I attach to them—has been holding me back from working with the deep heart of what is really going on inside of me, and what is really possible within me, as I experience the charge.

Hmm.

As I sit there in class, I feel myself fighting against this idea, even as it (sort of) excites me to hear it stated. Extreme anger seems so different to me from deep regret. And both seem wildly divergent from someone shut down and depressed, immobilized within themselves. How odd, then, to begin thinking about these experiences not in terms of how contrasting they are (especially as they appear to us on the Logistical Level), but rather in terms of what makes them the same. How curious, to begin allowing myself to see these experiences more fully, through the lens of the Essence Level.

I'm sitting there putting the pieces together. I am getting it: that somewhere within me is a "center," a core, a resonant, peaceful, already-healed-without-needing-to-be-healed place. And that a charge within me might be some kind of alert system announcing that *my consciousness has somehow fallen out of alignment with that center.*

Hmmm.

This would mean that the feeling of "charge" is not necessarily a bad thing. Especially if you know how to work with it. And the reality is, we are incarnated here as human beings, not robots. The idea of walking around NOT feeling a charge on anything is pretty absurd. And, anyway, it would be boring.

But even so it is a bit of a world-rattler to think of upsets as something other than bad. We have been so conditioned to think of upsets as something we should avoid. It's exciting and strange to consider viewing my own past experiences of anger, judgment, or disquiet through some new lens that is more about healing than it is about me *blowing it* or me *getting knocked edgewise* by some person or event. Is it possible that all the "charged" moments in my life were a gift of some sort, inviting me to open some package deep within myself, so that I could know myself better, tend to myself more fully, and come at the world from a more healed and healing place? And if so, how would that work? What was I missing when I was just getting upset and not "working with it" in some productive way?

My skeptical mind began to rebel. *But wait*, it said, *this can't be right. Aren't we all supposed to be "holding it all together?" Isn't it better to be constantly compassionate, like Mother Teresa, or pleasantly non-attached, like the Buddha and Gandhi and the long line of other luminaries who got their butts kicked by life and then came back all happy and wise?*

Well, yes. Grace under pressure is a wonderful thing. And the ability to detach from outcomes and upsets is powerful and freeing. Aspirational. Inspirational.

But the real juice, if you ask me, lies in knowing how to USE any upset you are experiencing to expand what you know and to deepen your connection with yourself. And then to offer that knowledge and inner compassion to make a difference in the lives of those you come in contact with. And that starts, to the best of my understanding, in learning how to work effectively with the "excess energy" of a charge. So here is what you need to know:

Any "charge-energy" that is disproportionate to the situation is an open doorway: a giant invitation *inward*.

What is a "rightful" amount of CHARGE and what is an "excess" or "disproportionate" amount of charge for any given situation? Let's explore.

LEARNING FROM DISPROPORTIONATE CHARGE

Think about what it feels like to be driving along the highway and to cut someone off a little as they enter on a merging lane. You might not mean to cut them off, but the dynamics of the road might just push you over a little bit. You could speed up so as to cut them off slightly less, but traffic is dense—the car ahead of you is a little close for that. And, anyway, this is all happening fast. You have to make good decisions in the moment. And, besides, they are the one merging. It's their job to gauge when to enter, not yours, right? Anyway, let's say you do cut them off. A little. And for totally understandable reasons. But they don't know all this. What they do know is that your movement, as they are merging into your lane, was unexpected and they are suddenly rattled. And now they are taking it out on you. They are honking their horn. But wait! There's more! They are pulling alongside you. They are pointing at you. They are yelling something. They're flipping you off!! Now they're shaking their head, and now they are rushing out ahead of you.

This feels bad. You feel a sickly jolt shoot through you. Ick. Yikes. Yuk.

Now one of two scenarios is about to play out for you.

Scenario One

That was hard. You feel shaken, and the feeling is getting worse instead of better. You are breathing faster. Your mind is racing. You feel almost nauseous. You are knocked edgewise by the presence of this person you have never met before and never even knew existed only moments ago. You feel defensive, misunderstood, and, frankly, indignant at their behavior. You run the incident over and over in your mind. You check all your decisions leading up to the moment of the supposed "cut off" and they all look sound and solid. You review their finger thrusts and angry lip movements. This is increasingly upsetting. You try to put it out of your mind, but your eye keeps scanning ahead to see if you can see their car. Your hands are shaking. Part of you wants to pull off and hide, to find them and punch them, or go purchase and consume an entire chocolate cake. Forty minutes later, when you arrive at work, you are still experiencing a lingering toxic feeling throughout your body. You are "back to normal," but quicker to snap at others at the morning meeting. And you have an increased awareness of annoyances about little things like the coffee being frustratingly lukewarm. This thing has *gotten under your skin*. Blecch.

Scenario Two

feel shaken. You were doing the best you could. They that. They were hostile to you. You feel upset inside. imes, send a silent apology to the other person as d accept responsibility for your part in whatever d yourself you were doing the best you could, as were they. You can see the energy of this exchange clearly: Right now, that person needs to be mad at an unknown stranger. They don't have access to their own abilities to hold the experience in a centered place. You let yourself imagine that their upset might have had more to do with other things in their life than just your vehicular maneuver. You silently hope their day gets better from here. You clear a little opening within yourself to invite your day to get better from here, too. You breathe. You allow the tenseness in your shoulders to soften. You locate the upset place within yourself, take another deep breath, expel the experience yet a little more, and feel it moving through you to a kind of completion. Out the window you notice that some of the trees are starting to bloom. Pretty!

In both of these situations, you are experiencing a charge on what is happening. A charge signals that something is "off" or feels loaded. It has suddenly become harder to locate, access, or connect with that place inside of you that is peaceful, centered, happy, and simply floating along. It's still there, but your ability to connect with it is somehow compromised, or the attention and intention required to stay with it has been hijacked in the direction of the upset.

In both scenarios, you feel bad. In both scenarios, an upsetting thing happens, and then you drive on to work. But in the second scenario, the intensity and duration of the "charge" seem to be *commensurate to the situation*. In the first scenario, it shows up as *disproportionate to the situation*. The charge lingers on, infesting and infecting the rest of your morning. Why?

THE AMOUNT OF EXCESS CHARGE MATTERS

Let's look at the charge that is proportionate to the situation. Of course it feels bad to have someone scold you. It could feel bad for any number of reasons (it was a surprise, it's hard to receive anger, they misunderstood your intention). But your ability to put this particular experience into its larger context (he and I do not even know each other, we both are operating on limited data, no one set out to harm anyone, near misses on accidents can stir people up because they become frightened) can be measured easily in the way the charge jumps only a little and burns off relatively quickly, *as soon as you give it some contextualized attention*. It's not taking up head-space at all fifteen minutes after the incident.

occurred. It's a memory of an unplanned and uncomfortable moment that you can move into and then gracefully out beyond.

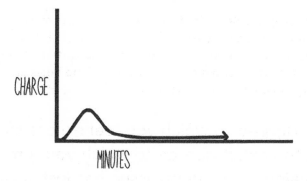

Now let's look at the charge that is disproportionate to the situation. This is incredibly upsetting to you. It's hard to get the feeling to pass. The way you feel bleeds into other interactions that follow it. It feels really disturbing to have someone yelling at you like this. You are upset and irritated on a level and to a degree that makes it hard to STOP feeling bad, even long after the moment has passed and the other driver has ridden off, cussing into the horizon. The idea of "talking yourself out of being upset about this" doesn't get any purchase within you, because the more you think about it, the *more* upset you feel. And the more you try not to think about it, the more you think about it. It does start to fade, eventually, but the fade takes a long time, feels awful, and seems more responsive to a good stiff drink or some other distraction than to any attempts to ponder it. It stays with you. It lingers for a long time. And it feels truly crappy.

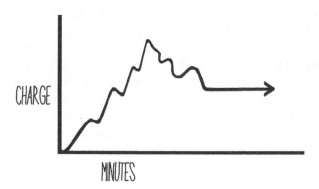

In this second scenario, there is an excess charge. And that charge seems to be having its way with you.

This can be really problematic. It feels awful *and* it can make your presence toxic—temporarily anyway—to others. It may appear that there is little to do about a charge that is "disproportionate to the situation" except to wait it out. And waiting it out IS an option. Time heals all wounds, and all that. But I invite you to consider this:

The degree to which you feel excess charge is the exact degree to which you remain *unhealed* on whatever issue has just surfaced.

Proportionate charge means stuff happens, it bugs you for a moment, and you move through it and keep going. Disproportionate charge, I am here to tell you, means something different. It means somewhere down inside you, an unhealed wound, an old unmet need, a place of hurt, confusion, or pain larger than just this moment and this potential annoyance has just gotten activated. The good news in all of this is that that excess charge is here to help you learn to heal. From the depths of your being, when a disproportionate charge appears, you are being notified that *something* on the inside is unhealed and is now "up" from whatever dark crevice it has been sealed away in until just now—until this exact triggering moment, filled, if only you will see it, with healing potential.

I invite you to think about a "disproportionate charge" like a scab that has just been ripped open to the stinging air. As painful as it may be to have this wound suddenly exposed, it is also great news that your awareness of it is now more present. Because you, above all others, are fully equipped to heal it. You, alone, were born with the entire "recipe" for the healing tincture for *this very wound, specifically.* You, more than anyone else on the planet, are the one who is uniquely qualified to mix and apply just the right salve to your very own laceration. You need only to be reminded that you have this information and this ability. And I am here to remind you.

SAYING YES TO PAIN

It takes a deliberate shift in consciousness to choose to work with pain non-reactively. It takes a deliberate shift in consciousness to turn to an ache and say "YES" to it instead of "NO." And—here's where it gets interesting—one of the hardest moments to try to make that shift is while you are standing in the middle of the firestorm of a disproportionate charge.

Why? Because a charged moment is a strange moment. In a charged moment, you are uncomfortable. You are writhing. The sting of the air on this newly scab-less abrasion *hurts*. You are not in the mood to be reminded of anything profound within yourself. You are upset. You are hurting. And the subtle whispers from deep within, of *"Look in here; look in here"* are, in this moment of upset, below your current levels of detection.

If you are like practically everybody else on the planet, you are not naturally inclined to turn inward at a moment like this. It is not necessarily your first thought. Your thought, if we can call it that, in a moment of excess charge, is rather singular: *MAKE THIS FEELING OF DISCOMFORT GO AWAY.*

That thought very quickly supersedes everything else.

Your subconscious now begins searching frantically for something sticky.

Quick! Formulate something, before another second passes: MAKE IT GO AWAY.

And so, you scramble to come up with a "stance"—a way to respond to this charged feeling (and your desire to make it go away) as fast and as seamlessly as possible.

RESPONDING OUT OF DESPERATION

This response—this stance you will come up with—is notably separate from the things you create with your regular conscious thoughts. You will create this stance not out of careful consideration but out of desperation. You will slap it together fast, from within the pit of your own discomfort. And it will be weirdly brilliant, this little stance, in one particular way. It will work. For now. Your subconscious will come up with this approach because it wants, in this moment, ONLY ONE THING, and it will grasp for it with no regard for any associated cost: Your subconscious wants to *make this discomfort go away.*

Without even really realizing you are making a choice—in a highly reactive state, and moving very fast and almost automatically—you will turn your focus not so much onto the hurt or pain you feel, but rather, onto your intense desire not to feel it, not to show it, not to have it, and not to have it known. You will say something, or do something. You will attack. Or you will retreat. You will lash out. Or you will stonewall. Or you will go through the motions of laughing it off. You will cry distracting tears. Or you will dissociate from someone, for the time being or for eternity, depending on the scale of the incident and the depth of your discomfort. In short, *you will try to disengage from the pain by engaging in drama.*

You will do this over and over again, in situation after situation. You will do it because it works. Sort of. It will, in fact, offload the discomfort of the moment. For a little while.

But ultimately, it will cause great pain, frequently to those around you, and almost certainly, very predictably, over and over again, deep inside of you.

This is the creation of toxic energy.

Your "plan," your stance, your response, from deep within a writhing, uncomfortable, overwhelmed place in your subconscious, is simply this:

I will form a judgment, or
I will create a story of blame, or
I will create a narrative based on fear.

Whether we are aware of it or not, this is what we do. And whether you are ready or not (you are—I know you are), it's time to look at what can be done to stop creating stances out of a desire not to feel, and to start learning to follow the energy of a "disproportionate charge" directly into healing and growth.

There are different approaches. Consider these:

I will become open to the pain.
I will release the stories I've been clinging to.
I will look for new learning.

To get there, we need to look closer at the strange allure of judgment, blame, and fear.

Chapter 10

Toxic Stories of Judgment, Blame, and Fear

I do sort of want to laugh at all of us sometimes. If you were floating 10,000 feet above yourself and looking down at *You in Action*, some of the stories you compose from the depths of your discomfort, to explain to yourself what is happening, might cause you to laugh, too.

Something hurts us and instead of saying, "Ouch, that hurts," we so often take the blow and then immediately break into two pieces.

One piece of us stays on the surface, where we are interacting with others, and that piece behaves in what we imagine to be functionally acceptable ways.

The other piece of us hovers below the surface, out of sight. That piece does everything in its power to immediately throw off the hot potato of discomfort. The net result can be really bizarre if you let yourself see it. People everywhere are hurting, but acting like they are fine.

NOT FALLING

I want to tell you a story about a two-second period that helped me understand something deeper about human nature:

I am eighteen, a college freshman, walking down to the football game on a rainy fall afternoon with six other young women. Over the first few weeks of school we have formed a little band, quickly Velcro-ing ourselves to one another as we adjust to this new environment, seeking to create familiarity and connection within it. We are laughing and talking and singing. As we walk, out of the corner of my eye, I see a blur. One of my new friends, Marie, has tripped. What transpires is so strange. Marie

is near the back of the group, and within a split second, she is down on the pavement. But then, almost faster than logic, before I even have a chance to fully turn my head and see her, she is right back up again. I watch her use every resource she has to *pretend that she has not fallen.*

She doesn't know I have seen her fall. She seems to think no one saw it, and that perhaps if she can right herself fast enough, no one will know it occurred at all. She has bounced up quickly from what looked to be a pretty hard slam and then scrambled to verbally re-insert herself into the flow of the conversation before she has even fully regained her balance.

She pulled it off. But it struck me as so … *universal,* this wish we all seem to have, to *appear* as if we are *not ever falling.* To get away with the illusion, if we can, that we are on solid ground, even when we are not.

It meant something to me, from that unseen, sideways vantage point, to observe Marie falling and attempting to quickly right herself, because I do this, too. We all do this in some way or other.

"No, no, I'm fine," we say, when we are nothing of the kind.

"What, this?" we ask. "No, it's nothing. Back to you. You were saying?..."

Without her realizing I was seeing it, I watched Marie make a very quick "swap out." She replaced one story (*I am falling*) with another (*I am a person who did not just fall*). She did it almost <u>instantaneously</u>. Like a bait and switch. The strange thing was, the first story was grounded in reality. The second story was fabricated *in one split second, right there on the spot*. There was no advance planning about this for Marie. There was no time for her to sit there and weigh the options. One full-blown actual moment in her life (*I fell*) was replaced with one full-blown not-actual moment (*I did not fall*). The new story was "sold in." But it was not real. She fell. I saw her. It probably hurt. It looked like it did.

So what place within Marie—what piece of her—wrote that alternative story? What part of us, within us, writes "alternative" stories *that* fast? And why? What was a story about *not falling* designed to provide for Marie? What are these kinds of stories designed to provide for any of us? Because I am here to tell you, we all write them, all the time. Some of us write them well aware that we are doing so. Others of us do so unconsciously or almost automatically. But it happens, in our culture, a *lot*.

I can't know for sure about Marie that day. I never asked her. She was working hard to have her fall not be seen, and it made sense to me to just go ahead and honor the illusion she was selling. But it taught me something.

HASTILY FASHIONED SUBSTITUTION STORIES

I believe that all of us, very quickly, very much on the fly, regularly compose stories designed to *hold our discomfort at a distance from ourselves.* I think we do this because we imagine that peering deeply into an unhealed wound might hurt us more than we can handle. We imagine that redirecting or masking an uncomfortable energetic charge is a better choice than looking directly at it with curiosity.

When it comes to dealing with discomfort and upset (*make it go away!*), it turns out we are all, in a wide range of ways, masterful quick-change-artist storytellers.

But these stories we tell are the strangest kinds of stories. The longer I have been in the business of helping people heal old hurts and unburden themselves from limiting beliefs, the more I have seen that we all, in one way or another, do something very odd when we are overwhelmed with what is happening around us:

> # Most of us fill in the missing pieces of an upsetting experience *from a place of pain.*

We literally single out the parts of what is happening around us that don't make sense to us, and then—perhaps because we can't stand the discomfort of events not making sense, or perhaps because we live in a culture where speed and certainty are valued over patience and curiosity—we quickly generate explanations for what is going on that are not necessarily in alignment with reality. We fashion stories, ways of making sense of that which is overwhelming us, *based on some painful, unresolved experience we have had in the past.* In this way, we "awful-ize"—interpret something that is happening right now as *more awful than it necessarily is.*

"I know what *THIS* is!" we say, working from a tiny little sliver of data. "I've seen *THIS* before! This is *BAD!*"

It's Rose, trying to make sense of why her ex-husband will not sit and talk openly with her about the unraveling of their marriage.

It's me, conjuring blaming stories around the end of my marriage.

It's you, experiencing the road-rage driver and trying to make sense out of why he treated you so badly.

The habit of assuming we know exactly what "this" is is a compact and tidy approach. It's the other person's fault. Now we get to walk away and go back to feeling however we were feeling before this person came along and ruined everything. (OR, for some of us, it's *our* fault and now all we have to do is apologize and never look any closer at *their* contribution.) Either way, we move *away*—which would be fine, if no pain lingered. But often, for them, or for us, or both, it does.

Why would we operate this way? What could these quick, assumptive, negative "replacement" stories possibly provide us that is better than simply saying out loud, "I don't understand what is happening right now. I am overwhelmed, but I am curious. What do you see? What do I see? Can we help each other fill in the blanks here?"

I think these stories buy us reprieve, in the moment, from the one thing that so many of us have not learned to tolerate: uncertainty. Lack of clarity. Not-knowing-ness. How fascinating that so many of us, in a moment of overwhelm, where all is not clear, will choose the idea of awfulness (*I know what this is—I have seen this before—this is bad*) over sitting even one moment longer with The Unknown, to make room for clarity.

When we are distressed, overwhelmed, or triggered, time and again, without even realizing we are doing it, we fill in blanks from a place of skepticism and pain. I have watched clients sit with me in my office telling me their story. When they reach parts that don't sit cleanly with them, they quickly plow right past curiosity and into "I know what this is and this is bad." When you are on the outside watching it, it hurts to watch.

When you are on the inside of doing it, I know from experience, it hurts in a different way. Because this kind of translation leaves a lingering toxic feeling inside.

There is deep value in learning to catch yourself slugging in a "substitution" story. If you can see it happening, you can Change Your Mind and make choices from a more centered place within yourself.

COMPOSING FROM PAIN

The cycle begins because we have access to a few pieces of information that we know are true. About the road-rage incident, for example, we might say that we experienced these three things:

We're right. We do know these things. But there are lots of other things we *don't* know. That said, in the tension of the moment, we don't generally tend to see ourselves as having choice. (*Hmmm. Should I deeply tend to the heart of the upset within me or not?*) Instead, we do something so immediately and so automatically that we barely recognize that we have done it: We *fill in the blanks about the aspects of the story we don't know* in the quickest, most pain-reducing way we know.

And so it comes to pass that, in a split second, composed by some wounded, hurting little space inside of us, we make a fast conclusion, fill in the blanks, and land on a narrative that ties these three concrete pieces of the experience together with one singular sweeping piece of data about someone we have never met and with whom we have had only six seconds of one-way interaction:

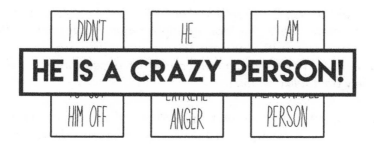

This interpretation of what has just played out is neat and tidy, and it does bring the whole thing to a seemingly "clean completion" because, suddenly, we are freed up! In these substitution stories, we don't have to hurt. We don't have to examine our choices, or the nagging question about what made us move before checking the lanes or move about as we wanted on the road without considering how it might impact the person merging behind us. It frees us up from the discomfort of this moment because it transposes everything into a black-and-white, two-dimensional story where there is a bad person ("crazy" man who yells and cusses) and a good person (reasonable citizen, aiming to do no harm, on his or her way to work).

This simple two-dimensional story also gives us someplace to focus all our upset. *Oh, man, you should have seen this maniac on the road this morning. Screaming and yelling over NOTHING.*

And, should we want to expand into our upset even further, so we don't have to look one iota deeper into why we make the kinds of choices that sometimes hurt other people, we can just keep going, wagging our finger at society at large. *What a crazy world we live in where everyone is trigger-wired to blow. Traffic should never be this thick. Rush hours are nuts these days. Our whole society is so messed up and this guy is a classic example of everything that is wrong, OUT THERE.*

This, I keep finding in myself and in those that come to me for support, is what we do. We write fast stories, on the fly, from a place inside of us that has a fear-based interest in protecting itself from looking deeper within—a desire to quickly find something dramatic and obvious (distraction, distraction, distraction!), outside of us, that keeps us from having to really explore inward.

What would we see if we really looked? What are we so afraid to know? Perhaps we are afraid that looking might require us to make different choices, step yet FURTHER into the unknown. We are, so often, so afraid we might have to reckon with ourselves, or see something that we genuinely do not like within us.

We do this fast-distraction-writing in zillions of ways, but I have found bolts of clarity in recognizing that these homespun distractions fall, broadly, into really just three categories: Blame, Judgment, and Fear.

STORIES FROM BLAME, JUDGMENT, AND FEAR

The stories we create to "fill in the blanks" are complex, intense, and drama-filled. They pretty much always have villains, and they consistently serve to keep us focused and aiming ourselves and our upset *OUT THERE.*

And, in just the same way that *anything* that has a "disproportionate charge" on it ultimately falls into the same simple category of UPSET, I would submit to you that ALL of the quick fill-in-the-blank stories that we compose from the depths of our discomfort boil down to three simple directives that keep us from having to (or getting to) attune inward and ultimately heal whatever is hurting.

1. **IT'S YOUR FAULT.**
   STORIES OF JUDGMENT (OR BLAME) OUTWARD
   You are the problem. If you would just change, I would not be hurting.
   - If you weren't so depressed, I could enjoy myself.
   - You never listen to me.
   - Stop being so passive-aggressive!
   - That group is too touchy-feely.
   - People who don't (or do) believe in God are clueless.
   - That candidate is an idiot.
   - **What stands between me and well-being = YOU**

2. **THERE'S SOMETHING WRONG WITH ME.**
   STORIES OF JUDGMENT INWARD
   I need to make sure no one ever finds out that I am deficient.
   - I am such an idiot.
   - I blew it again.

- I don't understand what's going on here, but I need to make it look like I do.
- I don't have the willpower to do healthier things.
- Why are others able to do this while I can't?
- I'm never going to be able to learn this, so why try?
- I am broken.
- **What stands between me and well-being = MY FLAWS**

3. <u>**THIS WILL NEVER WORK.**</u>
   STORIES COMPOSED FROM FEAR
   I'm in unfamiliar territory, I am stuck here in the unknown, and it feels awful. What's happening is bad and it's going to get worse.
   - I feel sick. I probably have cancer!
   - He hasn't called and he said he would. Something terrible must have happened!
   - If she breaks up with me, no one will ever love me again.
   - There is a tornado warning. Our house is going to be hit!
   - Everyone I know is getting a divorce. She is probably cheating on me!
   - If my daughter died, I would never be able to go on.
   - **What stands between me and well-being = THE BROKENNESS OF THINGS**

Most of us tend toward one of these sinkholes of thought more than the other two. I, myself, have gotten pretty good at letting go of blame and judgment. I have grown into seeing others through a compassionate lens, giving them a wider margin, the benefit of the doubt, and just generally more room to make mistakes and flail and find their way without having to be perfect or match up with my "standards." But fear stories can really nail me. I'm much better than I used to be, but I'm still working on it. It's worth taking a moment to think about which area is more of a pitfall for you.

Whichever area you tend to get caught up in, here is a thing I find fascinating: These three kinds of stories—*It's your fault* or *There's something wrong with me* or *This won't work*—all have, at their core, a marked *lack of curiosity*. The story is complete. The writing of the story is done. It is full of finality. After all, it was designed to get you off the hook, and to do its job effectively, there must be no open holes. It must be airtight.

But what if you are coming to know that "airtight" is stifling? What if "getting off the hook" is not your deepest goal? What if there is a trail to follow, clarity to access, relief to be had, and new levels of freed-up energy available to you when you expose yourself to a new way of navigating forward that is less about stuckness and more about flow? What if you learned how to reclaim the energies you have been fearfully projecting outward and frittering away?

Well, buckle your seatbelt because that is exactly where we are headed. You are ready now for the very strange (but ultimately very freeing) territory of Projections. And on the other side of Projections lies the opportunity to create the kind of inner dialogues that can truly change your life.

Chapter 11

Following a Projection

Perhaps you have heard of the classic concept of Projections in a psychology course somewhere along the line. With Projecting, also sometimes referred to as "blame shifting," the basic idea is that we humans, using our big fancy brains, have developed a way to *avoid looking at the most unpleasant aspects of ourselves by attributing them to others.*

Ever known a rude person who indignantly experiences everyone around them as rude, while appearing utterly blind to their *own* rudeness? That's the basic concept of Projections, writ large. But looking closer can offer us a lot more because, for people who know how to follow and then heal their own Projections, stuckness in interactions with others can begin to fall away, opening the way for greater flow, creativity, and authentic engagement with all the twists and turns in life.

AN INTRODUCTION TO PROJECTIONS

A Projection is a concerning behavior I can see in others but can't (yet) see in myself. Since I can't see it in myself, I have no way (yet) to work with it, make peace with it, or re-fashion it into something finer. Re-fashioning it is the road I'd like to help set you upon.

It's generally "easy" to spend my energy getting annoyed at what someone *else* is doing. It's a more uncharted, more gradual and careful ("harder") undertaking to stop and think, instead, "I may actually be extra-upset here because there is some way what I'm seeing reminds me that I have unfinished business deep within myself on some matter that is in some way related to what's happening right now ... but *how* is it related?"

In a few pages, I will show you, step-by-step, how to Follow a Projection. But let's set the stage with a concrete example:

Several years ago, I was in line at the supermarket checkout. In the next aisle, a woman was locked in an emotional tug-of-war with her toddler son. He was tired, cranky, annoying, and I could tell the two of them had had a long day together. He was begging her again and again for something (a toy? a snack? to get out of the cart?). She was rolling her eyes and blatantly ignoring him.

Then, all of a sudden, she was yelling. "NO! I told you no! No more talking. Shut up! Right now. I don't want to hear it. I've had it up to here with you. I mean it." The child continued to whine and wheedle. And the next thing I knew, just as I was walking out of the store, she hit him.

I was horrified. As I got to my car and reached for my keys, I saw that my hand was shaking. I was *really* upset. Understandable: A lot of people find it hard to watch physical violence, and I am one of them. But I was noticing my breathing was getting faster and faster, not slower, as I sat down in the driver's seat. I tried to reason with myself: *It's a terrible fact, but somewhere on this planet a kid is probably getting hit every minute. Of course I don't like it, but there are worse things. There's not a lot I can do about what just happened. It's not really my business ...*

Nonetheless, my efforts to put the event into some larger context seemed to be failing. Instead of getting distance from the experience, I found myself bursting into tears.

Okay, this upset seems disproportionate. But I can't possibly be having a Projection because I have never hit my kids. My parents never hit me. No one has ever hit me. I have never hit myself. So how can this be a Projection?

It took some attentive digging. But what I got to—sitting there in my parked car, crying, shaking, breathing deeper, and then taking hold of the moment and beginning to look more curiously—is that I was upset in some deeper, stranger way, about something in addition to that slap.

So I asked myself: *What is the specific behavior in that woman that I am finding so objectionable? What, exactly, is causing me to feel so deeply knocked edgewise? Is it seeing her shame someone she loves in public?*

Seeing her act out harshly, oblivious to how she is coming across? Seeing her get too easily triggered? Focusing her anger too directly on someone weak?

I took a deep breath. I held still. I kept searching. I waited for clarity … and, eventually, it hit me. I had been watching one person shut another person down *without listening to them.* For whatever reason, even though many things about that scene annoyed me, this one specific aspect of it had left me deeply—disproportionately—shaken when compared to all the rest of it. I had become unhinged watching one person "tune out" another person. But why would this particular aspect bother me so much?

I began searching further, with curiosity and gentleness now: *Has someone in my life "tuned me out" in a way that remains unresolved within me? Is there some way I shut someone important in my life down, without first really listening? My kids? My husband? Well, yes … I do this sometimes. But it doesn't feel like that's what's making me shake right this minute.*

Do I do this to myself in some way …?

There was a moment there in the car where time stopped. It felt like a door was sliding open inside me.

Ohhhhhhhhhh.

A whole world of awareness and clearer perspective started rushing forward. It was like popcorn popping—pieces of a puzzle coming together. *Wait! There's something here! This feels different.*

For many years, when my husband would take long work trips, a little voice inside me used to cry out for my attention—an annoying little frightened and upset kind of beckoning. It was a place within me that seemed inappropriately (annoyingly! embarrassingly!) afraid that something bad might happen to my husband in his travels that would take away our powerful connection from my life.

Looking yet deeper, I began to be aware that this place within me was still living with some buried, uncomfortable, un-tended-to feelings of abandonment from my first marriage as well. Despite my wonderful, laughing, cleansing ride on the dune buggies, and the good, hard work I had done to release and move on, there remained some little place within me that was confused, hurt, upset, and vigilantly on the lookout for the next possible form of abandonment in my life. Perhaps this part of me remembered other, earlier feelings of abandonment from childhood as well. Whatever it was, this part of me reared up and seemed unsettled, needy, whining, almost child-like, begging me for something (to be heard? attended to?) almost any time my husband took a big trip.

Childish. Needy.

Hmmmm.

As I stopped and really looked at what that voice was, and how I typically responded to it those days, it occurred to me that I would, in effect, do pretty much everything in my power to *not really listen to that needy, frightened voice.* While my husband was away, I would speed-clean the house, reorganizing closets and sock drawers, morning and evening. I would frantically, almost fanatically, arrange social engagements with anyone who was available. I would push hard within myself to look and act like the kind of laid-back wife who could easily handle lots of "husband travel" even though my deep inner experience was something triggered and painful. I would, essentially, *shut this little voice down without listening to it,* attempting to ignore or outrun it.

In my own way, I was saying to this inner voice, *"NO! I told you no. No more talking. Stop talking right now. I don't want to hear it. I have had it up to here with you. I mean it."*

It wasn't that mother's slap that set me to shaking as I walked out to my car (even though I *really* hate that that kid got slapped, and it really was awful to see). It was the vague sense that I was seeing something that was hitting *too close to home* (pun intended).

In that moment, there in the supermarket parking lot, I began to see for the first time, clearly, that I was someone who was engaging in something I consider to be an objectionable behavior: shutting someone down without really listening to what they have to say. The "someone" in my case was a little voice inside of me, but the dynamic was exactly the same as the one I had just seen between this mother and her son. I just didn't realize it until I paid attention to my (disproportionate) upset and made the journey inward.

This is something we all have the power to do—IF we can see it (which is the purpose of this chapter, "Following a Projection"). From there, we can heal it (the next chapter, "Transforming a Projection"). And once it is healed, it sets the stage for something amazing: a new kind of expansive and flowing ongoing inner dialogue that feels freeing and ripe with new possibility (coming up in Section 3).

In my experience, once I Follow a Projection, I can make peace with whatever was really going on inside me that got triggered. If I don't Follow the Projection, I remain stuck, getting triggered over and over again by what seems like a string of annoying people and incidents all around me doing all kinds of "unrelated" annoying things.

But what if all those annoying things *aren't* unrelated? What if all the upsets around you are cues and clues to help you find and send loving energy to the places deep inside you that hurt?

The journey of this question, and its beautiful answer, begins with waking up to the way Projections are everywhere, beckoning to us, all the time.

PROJECTIONS ARE UNBELIEVABLY PREVALENT

So how often are *you* experiencing Projections? It is my belief that any time (literally, seriously, *any time*) you find yourself suffering through a *charge that is <u>disproportionate</u> to the situation* (lingering, agitating over time), there's a Projection going on.

I know, I know. That can't possibly be true. There are all kinds of insensitive people out there doing all kinds of insensitive things that you have every right to get upset about that have nothing at all to do with YOU. But Following a Projection is a delicate and profound opportunity, and I want you to have access to its power. And to do that, I must ask you to *suspend doubt* about the prevalence of Projections in your own life and consider that being able to embrace and transform them, rather than fight against seeing them, will make you stronger, wiser, more centered, and much more *in the flow* in your life.

So what is a Projection? A Projection is …

- An unconscious reaction designed to hold a vague sense of pain or *discomfort with ourselves* at bay.

- A way to see an undesirable trait as *separate from ourselves* and "belonging" to others.
- A blame-oriented separation between us and a part of ourselves we have yet to fully see or understand.
- An internalized filter through which we see the world as a perpetual repeat of the same old hurts.

WHY WE PROJECT

So why would we do this? Why would we decide we don't like an aspect of ourselves, "cordon off" that aspect, then dress it up as someone else, point at it, and become indignant about it? If that sounds like just about the silliest thing in the world, it kind of is. But I have found that it's exactly what we all do, far more than we realize. And if we are doing it, and not conscious that we are doing it, we can get caught in some pretty unsettling and disappointing repeating cycles that are hard to break because it *looks* so much like the problem is coming from "out there."

We do this because we have become conditioned to do it, and because our culture reinforces it (it seems to make sense that others are to blame when we become upset). We do it because we have done it for most of our adult lives, and it has not occurred to us that it is a choice we are making and that we have other options. We do it because it has come to feel like a "baseline of normal" to us, to be in a reactive and therefore weakened state. We do it because we have come to feel that blaming will free us from the discomfort of the situation. And we do it because we imagine that taking full responsibility for our own disturbance somehow makes the other person "right," which might mean we have "lost ground" or will be exposed as "a pushover" or "weak." Finally, we project because we are caught up in the Logistics and have lost sight of the Essence of the present moment.

I don't think we do this because we *want* to blame other people, or because we *like* getting upset, or because we *enjoy* getting disconnected from a part of ourselves. I think, instead, there is a wound inside us that is unhealed and relates, in some way, to the Logistical upset we are experiencing in the here and now. It's a wound from our past. Not just a run-of-the-mill old upset, but an experience that was unprecedented, disorienting, deeply painful, and felt more overwhelming than our coping skills were ready for at the time.

Instead of *feeling* or showing or expressing that pain, way back when, we soldiered on through, pretending we had "not fallen," like my college friend on the way to the football game. We kept on moving forward *as if everything were okay, even though it wasn't.* And because of this—because of the way we were not able to stop and honor our own experience of hurting, deep inside us, a wound got formed. And the quicker we "blew past it," the more forgotten (unhealed) the wound became. If you stop and breathe for a moment, perhaps you can locate some moments, further back in your own history, when you felt one way (hurting) and acted another (fine). I think this happens far more than we realize, to our great detriment.

THE IMPORTANCE OF CIRCLING BACK

Now, I'm not saying that every time some situation causes pain you must fall down on the ground wailing in that very instant or else you will be wounded for life. Many of us have professional lives and public faces. There is a time and a place for pain, and many of us rightfully want to feel what we feel in private, rather than on display. All of this is fine. But if we soldier through, and then somehow do not *circle back* and navigate ourselves, soon, to a safe space where we can thoughtfully express and explore the true impact—complete with loving focus applied directly to that inner hurting or confusion or overwhelm—then we have just cordoned off a place within ourselves, and left it abandoned. We have just set ourselves up for future Projections.

Old wounds stay alive within us because of the ways we have turned away from ourselves, and keep turning from ourselves, in the face of our own hurting.

This is a critically important concept—one that seems to get lost in the shuffle in our modern-day culture of forward movement and putting on a happy face.

All kinds of things happen to us, all our lives, which hurt. We are beings, moving around. We bump into people. People bump into us. It happens. It's part of sharing a planet. The bumping is not really the problem. It looks like it is, but, having worked with hundreds of individuals stuck in hurt and drama for decades who are now moving around out beyond it,

I can tell you the bumping is not the problem. But what you DO, *WITH AND FOR YOURSELF*, when you have been bumped, turns out to be either the thing that lets that hurt resolve OR keeps it perpetuating inside of you unseen, where it becomes ripe material for Projection after Projection. You keep hurting, it keeps looking like other people around you are the reason, and the wound lives on inside of you, unhealed, untended, and unseen. It's not the bump sustained, but rather the *acting as if we are fine and turning away from ourselves in moments when we need ourselves* that causes all the trouble.

It's the parent who scolded you too harshly, the traumatic experience with intimacy when you were a teen, the job you got passed over for—it's anything where you "checked the boxes," acted the right way, soldiered on, and sped past the hurt and overwhelm too fast to ever really FEEL and TEND TO how hurt you actually were. It's that period of time *just after* something painful happens and *just before* you decide how loving and present you will be with yourself—in that exact moment and in the important moments that quickly follow. Following a Projection is about locating missed opportunities to be present for yourself, and honoring them now, because you *can*.

"How you relate to the issue IS the issue."

This basic principle of Spiritual Psychology, articulated so simply and uniquely by my teachers, Drs. Ron and Mary Hulnick, was shared time and again in my Master's program at USM. I ran headlong into this concept repeatedly, and its meaning slowly became clearer and more helpful to me as I began to dig out of stuck places within myself and set myself more and more free, emotionally.

How you relate to an issue IS the real issue and opportunity. Meaning it keeps LOOKING like the "issue" is some "thing outside of me": *the car accident, her attitude, his cheating, my terrible boss, the earthquake,* whatever. The real issue—the real cause of the turmoil inside of me—is the way that I either am or am not *choosing to stay lovingly present with myself* as I navigate through whatever is happening. How I am with myself as I navigate the issue IS the issue! And the skill I am about to walk you through offers a radically different way of clearing off past abandonments and setting the stage for a new way of "holding" for yourself, when you most need it, as any new challenges come forward.

HOW TO FOLLOW A PROJECTION

We Follow a Projection by noticing a disproportionate charge in ourselves and then staying engaged as we move through three steps:

- **Step 1: Isolate the Objectionable Behavior**
- **Step 2: Pivot and Turn the Mirror Inward**
- **Step 3: Ask Yourself, *Do I Do This?***

That's it. It's wildly simple, on one level. But it also requires you to break cycles you may not be used to breaking and to step into a softer, more connective mode in a moment of upset, which can feel wobbly and strange if you are new to this kind of inner work.

For most of us, especially those who are new to it, the time to work with a Projection is not in the heat of the moment but in a safe, quiet space, as soon afterward as possible. As you read through the steps below, some of you may want to "play along" by inserting your own recent issue and responses into the example I am providing. This can be a powerful way to learn. Others of you will just want to "absorb" the whole thing before trying it later.

At the end of Section 2, you'll find another SHIFT exercise, designed to help you with the most central aspect of working with a Projection: the sea-change moment where you stop blaming and instead pivot in a new direction and begin navigating down a road of healing. If you become masterful at that one clincher aspect of Projections, regardless of whether you decide to become a full-time Projections enthusiast, I predict that you will experience a significant transformation in your own well-being.

With that in mind, what follows in the remaining pages of this section is a chance for you to visit a process in which pain can be transformed into energy, and inner constriction can transform to a sense of purpose and power. Try it now, try it later, or just let your new awareness of the existence of this process lighten and expand your consciousness. However you decide to integrate what follows, I invite you to trust your inner pacing around seeing old limitations in new, expansive ways.

For the record, it is generally much easier to notice Projections happening in other people than to see them playing out with yourself (and generally much kinder to let others discover—or not discover—their Projections and for you to focus on your own).

Okay. You're ready. Let's work through the three steps of Following a Projection with a fictional sample:

THE TRIGGERING EVENT:
My cousin and I were having a normal conversation and then it turned into a fight. My comments felt reasonable and hers seemed extremely unreasonable. I got very upset.

STEP 1: Isolate the Objectionable Behavior

We start by focusing on what it was that the other person did that has you so upset. Interestingly, this is a moment where it actually serves you to indulge (in the privacy of your own mind) in wildly blaming the other person, because you can use the *specifics* of whatever comes forward in this safe space of exploration to help isolate the one behavior that is bothering you more deeply than all the other annoyances about this particular triggering moment.

With my cousin, I might rattle off this list, which could be extensive because I am upset:

- *She used a mean voice.*
- *She hit below the belt with all those comments about my new hobby.*
- *She was insensitive to me, and to everything going on around her.*
- *She never learns, grows, or incorporates anything we talk about after a conversation is over.*
- *She is incapable of having a meaningful, deeper conversation with me!*
- *She stormed off. That was so rude!*

The idea, in working with this list, is leaning into the notion that while many things she did upset me, one behavior in particular is activating me on a much deeper, older, more unhealed, unexplored level, and the others are simple annoyances. Locating that one objectionable behavior means "testing" the waters a little. Once you have your own list for your own issue, you can try reading off each item and closing your eyes after each one in order to pay attention to the charge within you. Does the charge grow as you focus on a particular list item, or does it soften and recede a bit? I invite you to work with the assumption that ONE of these behaviors is far more central to your disproportionate charge than the others, and that you can find it by sitting still and feeling your way into your own upset. As I go through my cousin list, I might say:

- *Okay, she used a mean tone of voice, and I didn't like that. But that's the kind of thing I could pretty easily understand and excuse, given the circumstances.*
- *She did hit below the belt with her comments about my new hobby, but upon reflection, I think that's because she has some misinformation about that. In a calmer moment, I'll want to share more info with her about it.*

Let's say I work my way down this list, tuning in, following the energy, and noticing that each upset starts to fade just a bit when I give it my full attention until … until I hit the item about "she is incapable of having a deeper, more meaningful conversation with me." When I land on this one, I feel furious. I am suddenly thinking of many times—MANY times!—when it seemed like she and I were going to "go deeper" together—get more real, connect more fully—and then all of a sudden she pulled away. *This hurts! I really dislike this about her! It happens a lot! Harrumph.*

I have hit an item on my list that can't be immediately eased just by my paying a little more careful attention to it and giving it some context. There's something more going on with this one. I can check the rest of the list to make sure this is really it, but in the end, I will return to this and realize that *this* is where my work, going forward with this Projection, really does lie. It feels different from the others. I have isolated the objectionable behavior.

I'll invite you to note that, for this particular sample, I have honed in on a "most upsetting list item" that is quite similar to the real-life issue that triggered me in the supermarket, in that both seem to have something to do with "tuning out vs. going deeper." I want you to know I consciously aimed for this similarity because I believe it will help your learning to follow this *kind* of issue all the way through to its healing conclusion in the next chapter. And it also acts as a nice setup for Section 3, which is a continuation of this very same topic—going deeper—and an overall theme of this book. But it's worth mentioning here that in a more exhaustive review of Projections, we might follow examples about any of an infinite range of potentially triggering issues.

STEP 2: Pivot and Turn the Mirror Inward

So now you have located the issue with the heavy-duty charge on it. Interestingly, Step 2 takes only a millisecond in Logistical Time, but it stretches out in countless directions with rippling wavelengths of clean energetic transformation in Ceremonial Time. It is the exact moment when you consciously step into your own power and see the choice-point that appears before you in the journey of this upset. Are you going to turn inward for healing on this issue or not?

There is a magical pivot point at the center of *every* upset. It's *right* there if you learn to look for it.

At an issue's pivot point, there are always two avenues available: exacerbate or heal your upset. When we slow things down and focus, these two choices become increasingly clear: I can *repeat* or I can *shift*.

(1) REPEATING – I can continue to fuel my old patterns, struggle to offload this all-too-familiar disequilibrium, blame and judge my cousin, justify my upset, and aim my toxicity outward (or even sometimes inward), OR

(2) SHIFTING – I can recognize that I am out of balance, that there is a "charge" for me on this upset that is *disproportionate to the situation*, and acknowledge that this is a prime opportunity to shift my attention inward and heal the hurt that is surfacing. I can choose to CHANGE MY MIND about how I am with this upset.

This kind of shift represents a small but mighty internal sea change. It tips your consciousness—in just exactly the moment you choose to let it—toward a more Essence-Level vantage point. It's an awareness and a decision, at a profoundly telling moment in your own personal narrative, that suddenly makes it possible for more to reveal itself and transform in new ways. It's the end of one way of "being with an issue" and the beginning of a new way of being, not just with an issue, but with yourself.

This is the pivot point.

It can make a huge difference, I find, to "anchor" this little split second pivot with something profoundly noticeable and hard-to-miss, on the Logistical Level. Here's the approach I like the best (though you could choose anything at all that speaks to you, like lighting a candle, taking a deep breath, closing your eyes, clearing your throat, etc.). I like to slow things down to the speed of self-love by asking myself one simple question:

**Am I genuinely willing to turn the mirror around,
to explore this dynamic within myself *instead of*
in the person who has triggered my upset?**

I find it most powerful to answer this question out loud, "psyching myself up" for the best possible outcome in terms of my own learning and healing:

I am willing to look at what my cousin is reflecting to me <u>about me</u>. I am willing to explore an aspect of myself that has been challenging for me to see. My intention is to bring this pattern into conscious awareness and to heal it.

As an added self-assisting step, when I do this on my own or am modeling it for a group or workshop, I literally pantomime grabbing a mirror that is facing away from me and then I painstakingly "act out" my struggle to turn it around and face it toward myself, letting the fight within me (resist? or grow?) play out in the muscles of my arms and face. I let all the resistance I feel about looking deeper show up, legitimately, as resistance to turning that mirror around. And I let all the places within me that are SICK of this pattern and HUNGRY to break out of it push *against* that resistance—back and forth, back and forth. I grit my teeth, I tug and twist, gaining a little ground, losing a little ground; f-e-e-e-l-i-n-g my way into the truth of all that lies inside me around making a space for change. I *groan* as I do it. I give myself the gift of experiencing how much resistance there is inside me and of feeling my ability to meet that resistance with an equal—and then greater—amount of desire to heal, to dare to change, to see more, to grow.

And then, finally, from that newly oriented place, I can ask myself: *Do I do this?*

STEP 3: Ask Yourself, *Do I Do This?*

So here is a truly amazing thing. When we choose to pivot instead of exacerbate an upset, *much more can be revealed.* In the *instant* we start moving down that new path, all kinds of clarity can be accessed within us that simply could not, as long as we remained trapped in toxically repeating, blaming, judging, and looking "out there" for the resolution to hurts most deeply embedded "in here."

Asking myself "Do I do this?" means asking, *Is there some way the dynamic I'm seeing in my cousin represents something unresolved, unclaimed, unexamined, and/or unhealed within myself that I am now ready to honor?*

It also means I am letting go of asking, "Is it okay or not okay if my cousin does this?" Instead, I can begin to say, "There is more I can learn about myself. This new learning matters more right now than the rightness or wrongness of what my cousin is doing. Learning it offers me more inner freedom, which is where I am headed."

The mechanics of asking at this juncture are simple. Since I was seeing my cousin as someone unable to engage in meaningful conversations, then I would now ask myself:

o   **Is this something I do <u>to others</u>** *but am not conscious of doing?*
o   **Is this something I do <u>to myself</u>** *but am not conscious of doing?*

With these two simple angles of entry, I can begin to bring a curious and loving light into areas that were previously obstructed within me. It might look something like this:

Do I Do This to Others? – I might begin to "sniff around," asking myself, *Is there some way that I have been giving the appearance of dialoguing deeply with others while in reality, I am holding some part of myself back? Is there someone in my life with whom I enjoy sharing but who I do not deeply attune to when they are sharing with me? Are there some important times or relationships when it feels safer for me to present a version of myself that I imagine others would want to see, at the expense of sharing a deeper truth, or vulnerability, or confusion?*

Do I Do This to Myself? – I can also check this dynamic looking inward, asking myself: *Is there some way that the conversations I've been engaging in with myself are superficial? One-sided? Is there some part of me that longs for a deeper level of sharing, communion, or expression on the inside and is not getting it? Do I spend a lot of time pushing* *forward, without checking in deeply and meaningfully with myself? Is it possible that my doing so is invisible and yet deeply painful to me, leaving me feeling left out of a valuable communion with myself, and therefore frustrated when I run into a lack of communion like that "in the outside world," for example, with my cousin?*

As I search in this way, I notice that I have a JOLT right here: "Do I spend a lot of time pushing forward, without checking in deeply and meaningfully with myself?"

Hmmmm. A kind of knowing is creeping over me. I HAVE, on numerous occasions, latched onto an agenda for myself (exercise more, splurge on a trip, or hit a self-imposed deadline) and bulldozed right past a quiet but balking inner voice, *without really listening*. I have often created a situation that is a far cry from a caring, meaningful, two-way dialogue.

And yet this is the very thing I experienced my cousin as doing to me!

(And oh! I see! *Because* I have been bulldozing myself *internally*, and *because* it has been a blind spot, it increases the likelihood that I probably do this to others, too, without realizing it. Maybe I even did it to my cousin while I was so busy feeling enraged that she was bulldozing *me*.)

In any event, the opportunity for change, it seems, begins right in this moment, inside *myself*. What would happen if I *advocated* less and *inquired* more when connecting with my deeper inner voices? Section 3 of this book looks squarely at this very question, with perhaps some unexpected and enlightening unveilings about what is possible when you invite your inner dialogue to come into full bloom.

People, including my cousin, do things that annoy and disappoint all the time. Most of the time we can feel compassion or at least neutrality about those annoyances. When we can't, the *heart* of our issue is not about them, but about something similar and unresolved within ourselves. And our ability to climb inside of that inner irritation and dare to look more carefully and lovingly *is where all our power lies*. Or where all our power stays stuck and re-triggered should we choose to stay locked inside the Projection, without seeking and receiving the gift of its offering.

But when we dare to Follow a Projection, we invite a new internal clarity and an accompanying rush of fresh, clean energy. All the power that we were dissipating through being upset with someone else is now available to us for Transforming a Projection—literally altering it with our own power from something toxic into something healing! And that's exactly what we're moving into next.

Chapter 12

Transforming a Projection

The sense of discovery and surge of energy that come from Following a Projection can have a powerful impact on your engagement with yourself. But please don't stop there. Much deeper healing is available now. It's one thing to discover that you have an unattractive pattern you've been blind to. It is another thing entirely to continue focusing on that new awareness with curious and healing energy. Now is the moment to invite the place within you that has been pinched and clinging—associated with shame, abandonment, or pain—to be seen in a cathartic, possibility-oriented light. This is the joyful art of Transforming a Projection.

Transforming a Projection means reframing and reintegrating a toxic inner pattern you had previously been blind to in a way that leaves you feeling more peaceful.

Changing Your Mind about what's worth getting upset about, how much or how little power you have, and what you are capable of creating in your life is *almost impossible when you are projecting.* But it's almost impossible *not* to think more freely, expansively, and proactively once you have carefully and thoroughly Transformed a Projection.

> Changing Your Mind means
> releasing the kind of righteous certainty
> that keeps you pointing a finger outward
> and missing the full journey inward.

It means learning to recognize a pivot point, and having the courage to say, after all you have invested in the opinionated story you built at that pivot point, *I don't definitively know what I thought I knew. And "what I thought I knew" has been making me unhappy.*

All of this hinges on your decision to Transform a Projection. This is the "work"—the gift, the opportunity—of letting what you have identified (this aspect of yourself that was *so* challenging to look at that you projected it onto another instead) guide you to a more peaceful way of being internally.

HOW TO TRANSFORM A PROJECTION

The transformation process happens in three steps:

- **Step 1: Accept the Pattern in Myself**
- **Step 2: Initiate Self-Forgiveness**
- **Step 3: Choose a Higher-Frequency Thought**

Before I take you through the steps, I think it's wise to take a moment to check in about your readiness. Ask yourself, "Is it *conceivable* to me that looking closely at distasteful patterns within myself could heighten my sense of well-being? Do I choose to stay open to examining what is objectionable instead of 'bracing' myself or falling into old patterns of shutting myself down against things happening inside of me that I don't understand?"

And, too, you can ask yourself, "Am I willing to let myself be lifted out of the judgments and limiting thoughts that have held me in this place of reactivity, projection, and upset? Am I inclined to simply exchange feeling judgmental toward someone else for becoming judgmental toward myself as I turn inward? Or will I let myself truly transform this energy of judgment into something that lifts me to a higher place, with the potential to lift others as well?"

These are not small considerations. These are focused, magical Moments of Truth in your life—sparkling gems of growth and possibility—that can help you decide who you are capable of being, and discover how it can FEEL when you start to joyfully BE that.

Being *truly present* and awake to this kind of journey is what makes it possible for you to begin to tap into the Deeper YES: that place that smiles within you when you are offered the purest and kindest invitations to grow, deepen, and expand. When you ask within—open, vulnerable, curious, and ready to lean into what is possible, not forcing an answer but embracing whatever comes forward within you—magical things can begin to happen.

STEP 1: ACCEPTING THE PATTERN WITHIN MYSELF

The first step is to *accept* this newly visible objectionable behavior or pattern *without making yourself "wrong" for having it.*

First, look squarely at the behavior. You could journal, take some quiet time out, or even use this book with a caring friend. Picking up on my Projections with my cousin (or even my Projection with the woman in the supermarket), I might say: *Okay, it's true. I sometimes bulldoze past resistant or concerned voices within myself. I sometimes create the illusion that I am "checking in" with myself before I proceed with my next step, but in reality I don't really go deep, get curious, or engage in a meaningful internal dialogue. This may very well be a repeating pattern for me, and one that I have not been ready to look at until now.*

Next, resist any urge to flagellate yourself over this behavior and instead practice the art of simply seeing it—like a scientist rather than a contest judge—as something specific, finite, measurable, and observable. Perhaps this behavior, upon consideration, has a certain vibration, color, shape, or symbolic association. (*It looks like a thin, shaky, yellow coating over everything I do.*) Maybe *you* are aware of a body sensation associated with it (*stiffness, mind feeling fuzzy or blank, adrenaline rush*). Perhaps you can locate times throughout your life where this pattern has played out. (*It happens when I get excited and just want to move forward.*)

Now as you get an increasingly clear handle on it, lean into the idea that this pattern is something you have chosen to DO (whether you were conscious of the choice or not) rather than something that you ARE.

Working with a Projection means clearly separating my worth as a person from the pattern I have been repeating.

Separating "my worth" from "my pattern" means holding two distinct ideas in your consciousness at once:

1. *I am a valuable, worthy, loving, caring person.*

   AND, SEPARATELY,

2. *Something has become newly visible to me: I often don't fully tune in to myself, even though I tell myself I have.*

Can you hold both at once? What does it feel like to see yourself as (a) valuable AND ALSO (b) capable of doing something you are not proud of? Can you look squarely at both *without justifying, turning away, denying, or minimizing the negative impacts of this choice?* Allow yourself the rare and empowering experience of looking back and forth, back and forth, between the two: *I am solid; I am good; I am a loving being.* And, separately, but also visible now: *That's what I look like doing something that's hard to watch; that isn't how I like to think of myself.* Both can be true. *I can accept myself as a worthy being, and also accept that this unfortunate pattern has been playing out within me, right under my nose.*

Seeing both your beauty and your problematic choices, without making yourself wrong, is the starting point for change.

I invite you to take a moment to close your eyes and try a simple version of this step: Ask yourself, *Can I see ways that a behavior that upsets me in someone else could represent a blind spot for me in my own behavior? And if so, can I see that clearly without losing sight of my own worth as a person?*

STEP 2: INITIATING SELF-FORGIVENESS

The next step involves moving directly into Self-forgiveness using a tool called "sentence stems." As simple as this tool may appear, though, there is a twist to using it in this case—a twist we've been building toward all along. Let's see if we can break it down:

Using Sentence Stems – A sentence stem is the first half of a sentence for which you compose your own ending. In this case, the stem is, "I forgive myself for _____." This tool is most potent when you use it 5-10 times in a row, in real time, out loud, coming up with different aspects of the objectionable behavior to forgive yourself for each time. It happens in a free flow, without stopping to edit or refine: "I forgive myself for A. I forgive myself for B. I forgive myself for C ..."

Tapping Into a Feeling Place – Softer feelings (shame, hurt, sadness, confusion, or disillusionment) are needed to help you do the deepest and most transformative work coming up in Step 3. But these are generally *protected* feelings, so not always easy to access on command. I don't know about you, but for me, simply willing myself to feel vulnerable doesn't magically play out as I'd wish most of the time. I can't always conjure vulnerability and softness right when I want to. But using sentence stems really can help unlock and unblock softer feelings.

Most people feel awkward about using sentence stems. But oddly, part of this tool's power is using it *before you feel ready*. The act of moving through one sentence completion after another, without pausing, often helps shift the internal energies from a rather methodical, robotic start into a much softer feeling place within.

As I move through sentence completions like this and assist others to do the same, something sweet usually begins to happen. Those softer emotions begin to rise up and meet the Self-forgiveness phrases that started out as "just words." There is a shifting and a loosening. I notice a sense of inner spaciousness, and an expanding connection to the Essence Level, where energy is more free-flowing, originating in the simple desire each of us has to simply connect and belong.

The Twist – That said, with nearly everyone I've worked with (myself included), there is a critical "rookie mistake" with Self-forgiveness that can quickly pull healing, tenderness, and Essence-access dramatically off course. Most of us mistakenly assume that Self-forgiveness is about forgiving ourselves for engaging in the objectionable behavior (as in: "I forgive myself for not tuning in deeply").

This approach almost never works.

We must learn, no matter how many false starts it takes, to forgive ourselves not for the behavior in question but *for the judgment we have placed upon that behavior.*

Behaviors and Judgments – We are glorious creatures, roaming around this planet encountering things—cozy things, sharp things, things that feel amazing in superficial ways, things that feel amazing in deep ways. Things that looked alluring but feel awful upon contact. There is nothing wrong with any of this! It's how we move; it's how we love; it's how we learn; it's how we grow. But the moment we begin developing and harboring (and feeding and hiding) *judgments about* the things we do, the world (inside and all around us) becomes a very contracted, altered, contorted, pinched-off place. It's the judgments—not the missteps—that need to be lifted off in the name of healing. Working with sentence stems *in a manner that focuses on the judgment rather than on the behavior* softens us so that we can work deeply and heal our unhealed wounds.

Clearing Off Judgments – Altercations, disappointments, upsets, misunderstandings, and even plain old laziness—all of these things happen. We bungle things from time to time. We knock other people off-center, often without meaning to. Others sometimes do the same to us. When we embrace this reality, we can look thoughtfully at what happened, feel what we feel, learn something new, get back up, and keep going, applying what we learned until we hit the next bump. It's completely understandable that we might bumble into *all kinds of things* that don't play out well (even patterns we repeat, unconsciously, for a really long time). It all works fine as long as we are willing to move into the forward flow of a learning mode, instead of descending into judgment.

And when we DO move into a judging mode, that's fine, too, as long as we know to pull the judgment back off *as soon as we realize we're doing it.* Because then we can keep going—keep learning, keep loving, keep embracing our mistakes and authentically seeing and sharing Who We Are.

It's not the objectionable behavior that causes debilitating Projections to form inside us, but our judgments about that behavior.

The "crime" is not that we are sometimes callous, un-attuned, or afraid. The "crime" (not really a crime at all, but a great waste of our precious life energies) is all the judgment, negative opinions, camouflaging (from others and from ourselves), and shame that coils around inside us and makes us weaker, smaller, more reactive, and more prone to drama and deceit—sometimes on subtle levels, and sometimes on very pronounced ones.

Forgiving Ourselves – Self-forgiveness is the process of carefully separating out behaviors from the judgments we have unconsciously fastened onto them during bumps along the way. Self-forgiveness is when we resist the temptation to say, as in the case of Following the Projection with my cousin, "I forgive myself for not tuning in deeply" and INSTEAD clearly state:

> "I forgive myself **for judging myself** as bad (unloving, uncaring, unwise, un-evolved, etc.) for not tuning in to myself more deeply until just right now. I don't need to judge this behavior. I didn't even consciously realize I was doing this. Now that I can see what I have been doing, I can make a different choice. There is no value in my having a judgment on any of this. It only darkens things within me and saps me of the energy I need to see myself clearly and to lean into new choices that feel better."

Understanding the difference between "I forgive myself for X" and "I forgive myself for *judging* X" is where all the healing power lies.

With my cousin (and with the Projection I was bouncing off my cousin), I can begin to see that it is the judgments that have been causing all the chaos—blocking my general feeling of goodwill, of expansiveness about myself and those around me. It's the judgments that are pulling me toward upsets—toward friction around how I think things "should" be versus how they are. I can begin to release that tension, a bit at a time, with each heartfelt, authentic expression of Self-forgiveness.

The Original Projection – Looking at some of my original complaints about my cousin (insensitivity, inability to go deep, inability to learn) I can now revisit them in a new light:

- I forgive myself for judging.
- I forgive myself *for judging my cousin* as insensitive.

- I forgive myself *for judging myself* as insensitive.
- I forgive myself *for judging my cousin* as unable to learn.
- I forgive myself *for judging myself* as unable to learn.
- I forgive myself *for judging my cousin* as unable to go deeper in meaningful dialogue.
- I forgive myself *for judging myself* as unable to go deeper in meaningful dialogue.

This process is inspired by what I experienced and practiced at USM. It helps delineate a critical moment in the process because we are in effect saying: "I am letting the behavior (insensitivity, inability to go deep, to learn) become more and more understandable as something that any good, caring person (including my cousin) *might* have gotten caught up in." And I am simultaneously recognizing that the way I have viewed this behavior (how I relate to the issue *IS* the issue) has been draped in judgmental energy. THIS is the sticking point. I can accept the behavior as something I (or my cousin) did in that moment, because we were each doing the best we could. I can also understand and accept that what she did in that moment was not a strong fit with what I wanted right then.

Generally, once we begin with sentence stems, new Self-forgiveness possibilities start spilling out. And often, with new relief and clarity, so do some cleansing tears.

- I forgive myself for judging myself as unworthy of the love of those around me.
- I forgive myself for judging myself as being unable to really see myself and others around me clearly.
- I forgive myself for judging myself as unworthy of kind, gentle, careful treatment from myself.

From deeper and deeper within, tangled, suppressed old aches begin to sense a safe opening and rise to the surface for healing. We are softening. We are honoring the places within us that have been hurting. Space is getting cleared within us for higher-frequency thoughts to enter in. I am releasing my unfruitful compulsion to judge. I am clearing out my need to see my cousin, or myself, through the lens of *bad intentions*. And I am ready to re-frame my thinking in light of the healing that is occurring.

STEP 3: CHOOSING A HIGHER-FREQUENCY THOUGHT

In my experience, when I have Transformed a Projection—located the judgments and then worked to release them to set myself up for cleaner, higher-frequency lines of thought—I will often find that ONE forgiveness statement will strike a particularly profound chord within me (e.g. *I forgive myself for judging myself as sneaky for not diving deeper with myself*). I have landed on something powerfully in need of healing, and I will often be moved to tears simply hearing this kind of inner acceptance and tenderness spoken out loud. Frequently, as the healing starts to happen, new thoughts will appear in my mind: related memories and related parts of the pattern. This, too, feels cleansing and good.

The disturbance is getting cleared. Therefore what's also getting cleared is any need to cultivate thoughts that rationalize my behavior (*What's the big deal? So what if I don't go any deeper within myself?!*) or beat myself up over it (*I keep claiming I want to go deeper but I never do it! What's WRONG with me!?*). Instead, I can now ascend to a higher-frequency, judgment-free level of thought. I can communicate directly with myself, lovingly, from a place of acceptance and understanding:

> *I see you. I see that going deeper has sometimes been challenging for you. It's OKAY that this is challenging. It's understandable. It's nothing you have to hide or deflect from any more. I embrace all of you, even the parts of you that feel really challenged or frightened at the thought of going deeper. Eventually, with love and support and encouragement, if you want to learn to go deeper, I feel sure together we will learn to create more of exactly this.*

"The Truth Is ..." – I use a very simple structure to help Transform Projections into their most exalted state. I start with a limiting interpretation of reality and then replace it with a newly revealed truth:

*   "I've been buying into the limiting interpretation of reality that is X."
*   "The truth is Y."

Some of the most gorgeous healing I have seen has come out of the simple, surprising "flips" that pop into people's minds when they dare to state a limiting interpretation of reality out loud and then replace it with a more expansive insight.

With my cousin Projection, which we can perhaps now reframe as my "Not Going Deeper With Myself" Projection, it might go like this:

- **Limiting Interpretation of Reality** – People will interact with me based on my idea of what loving behavior is. If they don't, that's evidence that they don't love me and are trying to hurt me.
- **The Truth Is** – People do what they do. They aren't mind readers, and they aren't always going to do things that look like what I would do in the same situation. Just because someone does something that appears uncaring to me doesn't mean that they don't care, or that it isn't a great opportunity to learn more about love in all its forms. Growth and love are not always comfortable, and that's okay.
- **Limiting Interpretation of Reality** – If someone does not appear to be "going deep" with me in a conversation, it means they feel negatively about me or that they are deeply flawed in some way.
- **The Truth Is** – A deep conversation is created by two people, and is very much about the ability of each of those people to "find" the other. When a deep conversation happens, it's a profound gift. When it does not happen, I can ask for it more openly; I can adjust my ability to attune to the other *where they are*, as opposed to trying to get them to come to where I am. Or I can seek a deep conversation elsewhere. The truth is, when I am most hungry for a deep conversation with another, it may be a flag that I am missing a powerful opportunity to have a deep conversation with myself.
- **Limiting Interpretation of Reality** – I can't really access the deepest places within me. It's too hard and I'm too damaged.
- **The Truth Is** – I am beautifully designed to "go deep" within myself whenever I say YES to turning inward. And I can start saying YES right this very minute.

I get that these revelations may feel advanced—the kind of deeper clarity that might come forward only after lots of practice. And I agree that more practice is good. But the reality is, I have been present many times when someone entirely new to the process opens their mouth to say, "The truth is ..." and suddenly a new level of consciousness and expression starts flowing out of them. What I hear in moments like these often makes me gasp. It frequently causes tears to roll down my face. When someone reaches this level of clearing, I find that what comes out of their mouths and hearts is consistently inspired, profoundly healing, and breathtaking.

When we are at this point, it is good to check in, over and over again: "What's present for me now?" The more we continue to ask this, the more we can learn.

Eventually, this kind of healing will bring itself to a completion in any of the following forms:

- A long, deep exhale
- A sparkle in the eye
- Peace, relief, laughter
- Option-generation, ideas, a broader sense of possibilities, avenues, and opportunities to come at this in a different way
- The ability to reconsider a thought that was previously charged, without feeling the charge
- A warm sense of connection to those present

Consider this in sharp contrast to triggering scenes all around the planet where Projections rule the moment and the healing potential remains buried:

- Two people heading off in opposite directions—in a huff, hiding, collapsing, or self-flagellating
- Rash, reactive decisions and pronouncements
- Intention to cease communication, lower expectations
- Threats
- The perpetuation of pain, anger, anxiety, hurt, confusion, and disillusionment

AFTER THE CLEARING

Once we have Transformed the Projection, it is a healthy, helpful, rightful thing to ask: "How can I apply this learning to my relationship with the person I have been upset with?"

In the warm glow of a Transformed Projection, it's actually fun to think about what else might be possible with this situation that, before making the inner journey, had felt devastating, upsetting, infuriating, or embarrassing. Perhaps it's about re-approaching this person differently. Or letting go, much more easily now, of whatever it was you were trying to create with them. It may be about asking more clearly for what you need (an acknowledgment? more details?), or feeling ready to apologize for contributions to the problem you were not previously aware you had been making, or brainstorming together with this person about win-win solutions, or turning to someone entirely different to get your needs met. Almost always, whatever the new angle, you can begin to notice that what is different is *the place within yourself from which you are able to re-approach this situation.*

And this is the real heart of the issue, once we get the dramas that are "out there" (outside of yourself) out of the way. It's not just about neutralizing the upset and carrying on. It's about recognizing when we are hurting and insecure, and then being amazing for ourselves in the face of it. There is so much more to learn about how connected we can become to ourselves—how present we can be with ourselves—once that external drama is softened and released. Let's review what we now know so that we can move beyond drama to the place we have been heading all along: that place inside of you where a whole new kind of inner dialogue can begin to bloom.

Chapter 13

YES Right Now: Takeaways & Explorations

I'd like to bring us into completion on Section 2 by sharing some Key Takeaways and offering a SHIFT you can use to start experimenting directly with the most fundamental concept in this section: claiming your powerful ability to pivot inward lovingly when there is unrest within you.

KEY TAKEAWAYS OF SECTION 2

1. **THINGS GOING BADLY** – Sometimes things just suck. When this happens, it can feel like you have no power. But on the Essence Level, time and energy move differently. This means, attuned to the more expansive Essence Level, you can learn to stop for an infinitesimally small moment in Logistical Time—(an expansive moment in Ceremonial Time!)—and invite any "upset" moment to become something radically different: a moment *not* about getting "hooked" by drama but instead about *healing*. To connect more fully with Essence in an ongoing way, all of us can learn to work directly with *transforming* the dramas we kick up and get sucked into around us into something more Essence-oriented.

2. **INDULGING DRAMA** – Most of us are overly focused on issues "out there" at the *expense* of what is really going on "in here," deeper within ourselves. We get drawn into external numbness (repetitive, addictive activities) and intensity (drama) because the stickiness or the tug of these activities is strong. Being distracted in this way keeps us in a "comfort zone" that is familiar. But it also keeps us from feeling fully alive and engaged. Everything begins to shift when we learn to see these "sticky places" not as a problem, but as markers or flags pointing toward places deep within us that are off-balance and in need of our immediate loving attention.

113

3. **DISPROPORTIONATE CHARGE** – Upsets (anger, overwhelm, stuckness) are really just an energetic charge moving through your body. Sometimes a triggering event will unleash a charge in you that is *disproportionate* to the situation (a high spike of emotionality and off-centeredness and/or a lingering, slow-burn feeling). The intensity of this "extra" charge is the exact degree to which a wound inside of you is unhealed, and is *sounding off* to get your attention. But it takes a deliberate shift in consciousness to work with excess charge non-reactively. What most of us do instead, as a default, is lash out at another or draw inward. And in so doing, we create the toxic, stuck-making energies of judgment, blame, and fear.

4. **OPTION #1: FEED THE UPSET** – <u>Any time</u> we are experiencing a disproportionate charge, we have basically two choices: (1) further solidify and feed the upset or (2) heal the underlying wound at its root. Most of us move quickly into reactive mode. Not wanting to appear wounded, we indulge and feed the upset without even realizing we are making a choice. Instead of becoming curious about what's happening, we create hasty, knee-jerk explanations. These fill in unexplained gaps by assuming that what's happening now is a replica of stories of pain and unresolved hurt that live within us from earlier wounds. These explanations, which justify and help us cling to familiar old upsets, show up as judgments, blame, and fear.

5. **OPTION #2: HEAL THE UPSET** – We can make a different choice. We can heal the upset by working with Projections. There are three steps to <u>*Following*</u> a Projection (Isolate the Objectionable Behavior, Pivot and Turn the Mirror Inward, Ask Yourself, Do I Do This?), and three steps to <u>*Transforming*</u> a Projection (Accept the Pattern in Myself, Initiate Self-forgiveness, and Choose a Higher-Frequency Thought). All of this together assists us in clearing out toxic energy within ourselves, and softening and expanding our perspective, so that, going forward, we can invite an entirely new caliber of inner dialogue, which we will explore next.

TRY THIS: THE PIVOT SHIFT

Everything in Section 2 has been designed to help you, step by step, to *acknowledge* how frequently Projections happen inside you, to *recognize* how toxic and stuck-making they can be, and to *own* how much power you really do have when it comes down to choosing whether you will fan the flames of the drama or heal the wound at the heart of it.

The actual steps of Following and Transforming a Projection are not hard if you are willing to take the time, and they get much easier with practice. What IS hard for almost everyone who works with Projections (or, if not hard, then at least requiring you to step into a really different energy dynamic) is the *very specific, utterly critical* 10-second period of time in which everything in you SHIFTS, a-w-a-a-a-a-y from the sticky, distracting allure of the upset (out there) and *gently t-o-w-a-r-d* curiosity and loving care (in here). THIS POINT, more than anyplace else in the process, is where you may need extra help and practice. And it's also where you can benefit profoundly from pivoting and playing with a SHIFT.

This PIVOT SHIFT can be used any time you are upset. That said, it is specifically designed to be used at that very particular point in the process where all the energy needs to begin flowing in a different direction with a different vibration. It's that moment where the energy must start flowing inward instead of outward, in a careful, curious way, instead of a judging, blaming way, so that you stop fanning the flames and heal. The SHIFT we're about to look at takes only a few seconds. It breaks the Projection cycle *just long enough* to help you re-track yourself in a direction of stronger, more conscious, loving choices.

This PIVOT SHIFT, like the ESSENCE SHIFT before it, is designed to help you consciously activate a *small* internal movement that can make a *big* difference to the energies around you. It is you who determines which upsetting events will "hook" you (keeping you outward-focused and off-center) and which ones you will tend to more deeply (turning inward for growth and healing). The key lies in creating a space within yourself where energies can shift, so you can begin to Change Your Mind.

THE PIVOT SHIFT:
5 STEPS FOR CHANGING YOUR MIND

Try this SHIFT whenever you feel upset or triggered.

1. **Recognize an Upset** – Recognize that you are feeling upset (triggered, off-center, angry, frozen, overwhelmed) and oriented toward something outside yourself.

2. **Set a Centering Intention** – State aloud (or silently) your clearest expression of wanting to shift the energy within you from triggered to learning and healing.

3. **Validate the Hurt** – Say aloud: "Someplace within me is hurting."

4. **Create an Energy-Pivot** – Say aloud: "I'm on my way!" Then heighten your body tension with intense muscle "squeezing" (arms, fingers, face) for five seconds and release, easing into a new energetic stance.

5. **Flow Inward** – Send loving, curious energy inward, aimed at any place within you that might be hurting. Wait for a response. Consider anything at all that comes forward as sacred and healing.

In the new, clean space opened up by the *absence* of projecting, it takes very little focus or effort for us to think higher and more loving thoughts, because it is our natural state to do exactly that. We are brilliant, gorgeous beings with the full capacity to see the greater context, tap into the Essence *and* the Logistical Levels at the very same time, and clearly take in the loving Essence within ourselves and those around us. We were born for this. And one of the single biggest impediments is simply our tendency to Project, over and over again, rather than choosing to PIVOT at the point of upset. When we PIVOT, we can stop the pattern, release blaming energy, and journey inside to the uncharted territories of our being. When our heart and our spirit are given full audience and voice, *astonishing* things can begin to happen! So let's invite that to begin.

The hardest part is behind us now.

From here we dive in together to the wide-open territory of your truest, most rightfully paced, lovingly honed relationship: the one you have *with yourself*. I invite you now to learn how to tune in to the most beautiful kind of conversation there is. It's the one that's happening already, right inside of you, on your very own inner Essence Level.

SECTION 3

DEEPEN THE CONVERSATION WITHIN

YOU AND YOU

*"Talk to yourself
like you would
to someone
you love."*

—Brené Brown

In this section, I intend to show you …

How to understand yourself much better
through attuning to the wide range of voices within you.

How to partner in a new way with
the places in you that have been hurting
by discovering the precious resources
buried deep within the pain.

How to access and rely on your very own
focal point of clarity, wisdom, and power—
one that is completely unique to you.

And how to raise the
purity and the healthfulness
of the energy flowing through you,
all by

**DEEPENING THE CONVERSATION
WITHIN YOURSELF.**

Chapter 14

Places Within Ourselves

It took me twenty years of practice for a certain kind of clarity to slide slowly into place, and for me to see what I now realize I have always known:

The _quality_ of the dialogue going on inside each of us matters deeply.

The place _within ourselves_ from which we listen to ourselves matters.

The place _within ourselves_ from which we speak _to ourselves_ matters.

The deeper and truer those "places" within us are allowed to become, the more expressive, connective, and joy-filled our lives can be. And, importantly, the more we have to offer those around us.

It helps to be reminded, as we saw in Section 1, that there is expansive, free-flowing energy—on the Essence Level—to which we can cultivate a conscious connection, as this makes everything feel better and flow better.

It helps to understand, as we saw in Section 2, that we can lovingly catch ourselves in the act of _distancing ourselves from ourselves_, and that we can instead choose to orient toward growth within.

But the point at which all of this really shifts from theories into deep internal re-alignments is the place where the dialogue within us _comes alive_ in a new way.

The clarity of this can be breathtaking.

This is a book in which each little piece of the puzzle is designed to help you move toward one thing: joining forces with **the finest, truest place within you.** In order to do that—to know that place and to have easy access to it—each of us must come to understand what to do with the places we bump into, within ourselves, that are confused, resistant, out of whack, damaged, or disconnected. We must learn to see them for their deeper value, and to engage with them, beautifully, in order to extract that value and create a connection. And we can.

Imagine a world where each person checks skillfully inside—deeply inside, easily and effortlessly, in Ceremonial Time—before making a game plan, before responding to an upset, before lashing out, and even before offering a gift or suggestion.

Attuning inward is not just an idea or a concept; it's a way of being.

Making inner attunement a priority is not just a goal or a task on a to-do list. It's a new level of consciousness that comes from the shifting of a mental construct. It's a recognition that we have become habituated to respond to dramas playing out around us, *at the expense of* enjoying what is most powerfully playing out *inside of us.*

Deepening the Conversation within yourself is about living into a more expansive inner dialogue, not because you "should" or "told yourself you would," but because *everything feels better when you do.*

It's about learning what it means to invite beautiful, authentic, healing, and empowering conversations to play out, inside of you, in an ongoing and natural way.

We are all "in dialogue" with ourselves all the time, though most of us are not in the habit of thinking about this consciously or of inviting the conversations playing out within us to become more amazing, more attuned, more inclusive, more encouraging, and more oriented toward joy and momentum.

If the idea of "places within us" seems strange, that's because it's not really a Logistical Level concept. It's an Essence Level concept. We are talking not about a physical location—"in the lower part of my back"—or "behind my left ear" but rather about a set of energies streaming through you, residing within you, entering into flow (or stuckness) within you, even just in this very moment as you read this.

If you're going to learn to navigate these energies and to celebrate and work with the way they concentrate into energetic "constellations" within you, we're going to have to think bigger, and journey farther in. You're going to have to attune to not just one new voice but to many powerful, important voices that are alive within you.

Chapter 15

Many Powerful Voices

I have referred to this concept of "meaningful inner dialogue" more than a few times now. But what does it really mean? Who, within us, is having a dialogue, and with whom? Understanding this, and then bringing your awareness to it in a more natural and regular way, is a delightful and surprising key to joy, I find. It really can, as they say, change everything.

It all starts with being able to tease out the cacophony of "inner conversations" playing out within you all the time—so much, so often, and for so much of your conscious history that you probably don't even realize they are there.

VOICES FROM WITHIN A WALL OF SOUND

When my new father-in-law came to visit my family for the first time, he spent each morning on our screened porch, bird-watching—a passion of his. On the second day, I sat with him and took in the wild and familiar "wall of sound" created collectively by all the summer birds around our pond. On the third morning, Bob pointed out the very distinct call of something called a catbird. What a fascinating sound—a bird that meowed like a cat! I told Bob I had never heard such a bird before. And he assured me that I had in fact been hearing it for years, as this bird was indigenous and clearly a regular in our yard.

These days, whenever I come out to the porch, I can hear that sound, distinct and unmistakable from the rest of the buzzing, whirring, and screeching I had heard as background noise whenever I entertained or meditated there. Imagine! Generations of catbirds had always been *right there*, sharing a space with me—indiscernible until I heard their unique voice distinctly; impossible *not* to hear, once I had.

It's the same, really, with your "inner voices." What I am about to share with you is a strange idea. But it has *so much power to it*, once you start dipping your toe into its full potential:

Each of us is filled with many distinct "formations" of energy, all existing at the same time, and in roughly the same "place," deep inside us.

Think of each formation as a little "being."

Consider that each being might be a character, or a personality, or a set of interests. Or that some of them might perhaps be more vague than that: a conglomeration of fears; or a concentration of energies oriented toward, say, the impulse to hide; or sensitivity to others. If it sounds like a gloopy, formless mess, well, it certainly can be. It's not unlike the "wall of sound" I heard on my screened porch for the first seven years I lived in my house in the woods. It was a beautiful, nature-filled wall of sound. But it had no meaning to me. *Until it did.*

In the Logistical world, to the extent that we are aware of this phenomenon of "formations of energy within us," most of us tend to think of them as "tendencies" or "aspects of our personality." There's nothing wrong with thinking about things this way, and, in fact, our Logistically oriented culture tends to reinforce this.

But on the Essence Level, if you let yourself become more fluent at tuning in, things begin to take shape in unexpected ways. You can "hear" and "see" much more of what is playing out inside you. With a heightened level of attunement, many new doors within you can begin to open. That's what Section 3, Deepen the Conversation Within, is really about.

For simplicity's sake, let's start by picturing these distinct energy formations inside you as little blobby beings:

Imagine them in there, chattering away. No one voice is particularly discernable. It's just a wall of sound, like a thick tangle of bird calls. You might find it beautiful, or it might be such constant background noise that you don't even notice it at all.

Whatever the case, I believe a fundamental key to your own well-being and forward momentum lies in your understanding of, and relationship with, these little "beings" present inside of you. I want to help you imagine that they really are in there. And then I want to help you interact with each of them in a more conscious way.

In order for that to happen, it's important for us to look carefully together at how each of these little beings inside you relate to one another, and how they relate to you. Why? Because of this simple but powerful concept:

> ## The *configuration* of the "beings" *inside you* has everything to do with how well events play out in your life.

MALLEABLE INNER CONFIGURATIONS

In my coaching, inspired by the pioneering work of Dr. Richard Schwartz, I refer to these distinct beings as Parts—relatively discrete subpersonalities each with its own viewpoint and qualities. It's a strange thing to talk "Logistically" about Parts, the way I am describing them, because they exist, really, on the Essence Level, a bit out beyond verbal description. They operate in a non-linear fashion. They live in a somewhat fluid state of being, in Ceremonial Time. They are various in their consistencies— they shift and morph as you develop and grow. Some appear, at times, in the forefront of your consciousness, while others fade, dreamlike, into the deep background. Sometimes one Part can take over almost entirely for a time. So, I'm taking a very Essence Level idea (Parts) and endeavoring to talk about it to you here in a Logistical way—with words on a page. On the Logistical Level, it might make no sense that "beings" within you might shift and recede, flare, or take over. But in the Essence realm, I invite you to consider that this is very much the case. Let's take a closer look.

Imagine, for simplicity's sake, that there are a handful of Parts inside of you (even though, perhaps, in "reality" there are dozens of them). For the purposes of this conversation, imagine that they are configured, rather randomly, something like this:

Some Parts are facing outward, can't see any other Parts, and may assume they are alone. Others can see a few Parts but have no idea that many others are right there, out of their line of "sight." Some might be deeply damaged, hiding in a box of their own making, where they cannot be seen, and also cannot connect or feel the warmth of others around them. One might be passionate, another needy; some might be good at connecting, some devoid of interpersonal skills. One might be "stuck" at the age of two, or seven, or thirteen, when some trauma occurred in your life that left them frozen or stranded while the rest of you "grew up." Some might be innocent or naïve. Others might be ageless, formless, almost like an ether, or an unrecognized place of potential deep within you.

In this strange, imaginary little world of inner energies, what each Part can see and factor in, based on where they are oriented and focused, has a lot to do with how harmonious or how non-functional they might be *if they tried to work together as a team.*

And this idea, of Parts all working together as a team, is a powerful notion indeed.

Ask yourself: What does the configuration of the Parts inside of <u>you</u> look like? Is it like a city street in there, with Parts passing one another by, not knowing each other, not particularly curious about one another, never having considered that they could connect in meaningful ways?

Is it a tug of war, with Parts grouped together on two distinct sides of issues, battling and exhausted, with a high level of energy expended and yet very little to show for it?

Or does it perhaps look like a loving circle of friends, joining hands, all connected to one another, facing inward, attuned, flexible, aware of the various strengths and trouble spots among the members of this little inner clan? This is a healthy formation:

CHARACTERISTICS OF A HEALTHY CONFIGURATION

In a deeply healthy configuration, there's no Part hiding or cut off, no Part facing outward unaware of being part of a team. No Part attempting to operate on their own, without backup, support, understanding, or buy-in.

In the healthiest version of you, there is wisdom and harmony, connection and *knowingness* of one another, among *all* the Parts within you.

In the healthiest version of you, when something uncomfortable happens "in real life," this circle of loving teammates knows, collectively, how to make wise and attuned decisions as a group, not just about what to do, but *who to help you be* in this moment. In the healthiest version of you, these Parts' decisions would be made not in the clunky, conflict-prone density of Logistical Time but rather in the ever-present, profound flow of Ceremonial Time.

In such a scenario, these Parts would know one another so deeply and fully that they would have a shorthand, much cleaner and more immediate, even, than the knowing looks, hand squeezes, and subtle nods we associate with well-tuned Logistical Level maneuvers. In a world of deep attunement to each other, they would gracefully slide into a new, rightful, impactful formation each time a challenging situation in the "real world" presented itself. In the Logistical World span of a single breath, they might simply all re-align, with the most helpful-to-this-situation Parts moving to the forefront, and others sliding quietly out of the way. In a healthy system with an inclusive configuration where all Parts feel well attended to, this is not only possible, it's the norm.

EXAMPLE: RESPONDING TO ATTACK

Let's say, for example, that it's you, operating out there in "real life," and that in response to something you have just said, your teenage daughter is screaming in frustration at you. She has hit a tipping point around the topic of your family's screen time policy—how stupid, unnecessary, and ridiculously restrictive it is. She is out of control and you can feel rumblings of upset reactions rising quickly within you.

In a deeply healthy Parts system, operating in Ceremonial Time, your Inner Collective intuitively knows what kind of Parts are needed for this exact situation. Without having to "think" about it in a Logistical way at all, four Parts slide into the forefront, seamlessly, and three or four others ease into the back, supported by the entire inner team in doing so.

The team sent forward to interact with your daughter's upset might include the following:

- THE LISTENER is curious and sharp—able to skillfully attune to what might *really* be going on for your daughter, underneath the anger.
- THE BIG PICTURE THINKER has the ability to see the larger context within which your daughter is asking. This Part can stay focused on the important larger questions without getting sucked into whether or not your daughter will like you five minutes from now.
- THE PLAYFUL GAMER not only *was* a kid once, but still is, and can still feel the lively vibrancy, hunger, and wonder of the experience of youth, *right now*. This light, fluid Part can see the discrepancy between what your daughter wants and what she has now, as a playful mystery to figure out.
- THE BENEVOLENT NEGOTIATOR is fully adult and understands that whatever solution you come to here needs to offer up a balance of support and independence. It's a Part that is not afraid to lay down boundaries, and also not too rigid or ego-driven to lift them. It's a Part willing to run a trial solution and able to have the follow-through to assess that experimentation after the fact.

PARTS THAT CAN'T HELP IN THIS CONTEXT

There are Parts that won't be helpful to "send up" into this situation, even though they matter and are not to be ignored, in the bigger picture out beyond this particular situation. Deep inside you, even if your system is healthy and well configured, some Parts may be reacting to your daughter's tirade with powerful energies that won't help you understand her any better right now. Those Parts are more likely to entrench you in old, toxic narratives than to help you both to grow, evolve, and become closer to each other.

A Part or two may be feeling defensive or furious. *How dare she talk to me this way!* Perhaps another feels unseen for all the careful work it has put into creating an inspiring, computer-free environment for your kid. Yet another might feel a deep, old, echoing ache. *Someone close to me is yelling at me again, and it hurts.* Maybe there's a Part that loves the excitement of a good clash of wills and can't wait to attack back, just for the blood-pumping thrill of it. Then again, some other Part, highly attuned to your personal productivity on the Logistical Level, is painfully aware that you already have too much work to do today: You don't have *time* for this conversation right now, even if it *were* going well. Which, it isn't, at least in the moments before this new configuration lines itself up and slides into place within you. Prior to the new, more conscious configuration forming, all kinds of energies are getting rattled up inside you. All kinds of Parts are gearing up: a fighter, a screamer, a shamer. Perhaps a crier. Maybe a hider. Parts that, in this *particular* situation, just want this awful interaction with your daughter to be *over*, and will do *anything* to try to force that to come to pass, without much regard for who might get damaged or what opportunities to connect might get jettisoned in the process. These are damaged, forgotten, untended Parts that need more attention (more on that shortly) before they can transform, need less, and offer more.

A healthy configuration—which I want you to have—means learning that your Parts can be interacted with and invited into formations that better serve. In a healthy configuration, your more unhealed Parts can see not just the "trouble" on the surface issue with your daughter, but they can see a wide range of other Parts down here, with them, as well. Unhealed Parts can know that more attention and understanding would be needed for them to be able to be helpful in this *particular situation*. They can see the other Parts that are more ready and able to help here. And they can slide into the background, *confident that healing conversations are coming their way*, in the not too distant future (though not now, during this fight, with this daughter).

ROGUE PARTS TAKING OVER

In a less healthy configuration, troubled Parts may experience whatever is happening up on the surface with your daughter, for example (or any other upset), in a very isolated way. They may assume they are alone, unobserved, un-validated, and disconnected. They may assume that the argument with your daughter is happening *only to them*. Often they are not aware that any other Parts even exist. They may be completely clueless about the idea that other Parts might be better qualified, in this particular situation, to help shape the way things play out in the screen-time conversation. Operating from within an unhealthy configuration, if one Part leaves the deep inner nest where all Parts reside and pops up to the surface to "deal with this situation," it is likely to be whatever Part within you is having the strongest *reaction*. And when that Part gets up to the surface of "you," to interact with your daughter, oblivious to other Parts that might have been able to help, it will tend to simply *take over.* And it will do so acting as "you." Not because this Part means to take over. Simply because it is wounded, disconnected, and uninformed. That's what rogue Parts do.

With a poor internal configuration, the situation gets hijacked during dramas and upsets by the least-healed Part.

Ever storm out of an argument wondering how on earth you managed to get so out of control? Ever resolve to eat more healthily, only to devour a mountain of donuts on the very first day of your new diet? Ever head into a conversation promising yourself to say nothing about topic X, no matter what, only to find yourself doing exactly that five short minutes later? That strange feeling of "returning to yourself" after the sudden derailment of your own intention and integrity marks the end of *One Part Taking Over,* and the system of Parts within you returning to its standard, default configuration. But it also marks the beginning of a lot of head scratching, apologizing, self-flagellation, and disappointment. The poorer the internal configuration of Parts, the less consciously all the Parts within it know and appreciate the strengths and wounds of one another. And the more often, unfortunately, painful derailments occur.

I don't mean to suggest that this approach (poor internal configuration, one unhealed Part taking over) doesn't ever move things forward. Sometimes, in the aftermath of all the chaos created by one rogue Part, new clarities can come forward and sweet vulnerabilities can surface. But what I want you to know is that there are more conscious, more integrated ways of dealing with your own inner configuration that are centered, curious, connective, and, importantly, *feel so much better* as you go along.

With me there remains, on occasion, an indignant, bossy-seeming Part that wants to make sure I don't get hurt. That part is all about protecting me, me, me. It lives deep in the story of the hurts within me that remain unhealed. This Part has a committed orientation to *not let a certain kind of hurt happen to me again, no matter what.* It has demonstrated that it has no problem yelling at a child or using nasty, guilt-inducing tactics to try to control the outcome of a dialogue.

I'm not proud of every interaction I've had with my own kids. In fact, there are a handful of exchanges that, if forced to re-watch in video format in some afterlife, I feel pretty sure I'd find myself desperately yearning to be able to go back and work more carefully, more lovingly, more honestly, not just with my kid, but even more foundationally, with that Part from deep within me that took over and hijacked, temporarily, the story of my love for my beautiful sons.

Most of the time, though—a joyfully high percentage of the time—I am pretty amazed at what comes out of my mouth and out of my heart when my kids turn to me with their upsets and challenges. The reason has so much to do with the configuration I have playing out within me, and the way I am able to *work with that configuration* in the presence of their upsets, and of my own.

MORE CONSCIOUS CONFIGURATIONS

Fortunately, most of the time, these days, I experience my kids' upsets as *distinct and separate from* whatever is happening to me, or within me. And with that awareness, I find that I am able to be curious and open with them, even when they are furious with me. I can learn more about what is really occurring for them (without assuming that I already *know*). I can hold a second reality at the same time and feel free enough to stay curious about what is really happening for me, too, even during moments of upset. Most of the time, I can draw meaningful boundaries to help my kids feel safe and heard and "at agency" (self-directed, operating from center) in their own journey rather than at the mercy of me and my "stuff" cropping up and taking over the situation.

I am able to do this largely because of the Parts configuration I enjoy *and cultivate* on the inside of me. These beloved little inner beings of mine have, for the most part, been well-listened-to by me throughout the months and years *leading up to* whatever upset I might be unconsciously heading into with one of my kids. This means the more troubled, still-healing Parts within me know they will be getting an audience with me once again soon, and are not likely to "need" to use the specific dramatic moments of my kids' upsets, for example, to act up, take over, or force me to notice these unhealed Parts by battling against my own unsuspecting young kids.

If that sounds like a new and unusual way of thinking about energies-on-the-inside, it's because it's a preview of where we are going next. And it all begins with some important fundamental questions you can ask yourself: What kind of inner configuration do *I* have? How conscious or unconscious am I of who's "down there?" How well do the Parts within me know one another? How united or fractured do they feel from one another? And, of course, most importantly, what do I need to know in order to invite and foster a healthier configuration within myself? You are worthy of a deeply connective, loving, and effective inner configuration. So let's look, specifically, at that.

Chapter 16

Strengthening Your Inner Configuration

The shift from an unhealthy internal configuration to a healthy one is completely within your grasp. I have walked this road with many a traveler now—some *desperate* to "get in deeper" and others hovering and resistant near the surface of their pain but fed up enough to try something different. In all this time, with such a wide range of individuals, I have come to notice something fascinating. There are, it turns out, five things people do that *work*, moving them from a weaker, more disconnected inner configuration to a stronger one.

1. Seek External Harmony

You strengthen your inner configuration each time you seek out and join in with environments, clubs, jobs, family gatherings, and even random conversations on public transportation that are inclusive, that are making space for vulnerability as well as strength, and that are unencumbered by drama or by a debilitating hierarchical structure. When you log greater amounts of time in harmonious gatherings, it becomes more and more natural for re-alignments to occur internally, even if you are not actively negotiating with your Parts to form a more conscientious inner configuration.

2. Turn Toward Callings

Every moment you do something that makes your heart sing, your inner configuration shifts toward health. All of us, when we stop to notice it, feel "called" in certain directions. The invitation here is to do anything at all that you feel deeply drawn to engage with or give expression to—anything you love to do that's not about what you "should" do but that's about *Who You Are*. Step into those activities (paid, volunteer, challenging, peaceful, in community, solitary) that allow you to experience yourself as fully *in the flow* within yourself, and do so newly conscious of the powerful impact it can have on your inner configuration of parts.

3. Constructively Vent the Pressure

Unhealthy configurations generally send too much energy to some places (some Parts get overused, overemphasized, over-favored, overworked) and too little energy to others (Parts that are unhealed, unseen, misunderstood, untrusted, or associated with shame). The more unhealthy the configuration, the more pressure it tends to generate (often experienced by you as stress, anger, disconnect, withdrawing, or agitation). The more pressure there is, the harder it is to coax Parts to shift into a healthier configuration. Therefore, one of the most immediate "assists" you can offer is to release some of that pressure. While venting does not get at the source of what's causing the pressure, it can help, but there are two kinds of venting: conscious and unconscious.

Unconsciously, when lopsided pressure becomes too great, our subconscious will conspire (brilliantly, it often seems) in conjunction with challenging events playing out around us, to create an opportunity for that pressure to "blow." When this happens, we explode, usually *at* someone else (often with a righteous rogue Part leading the way or taking over entirely), sometimes to very damaging results. Occasionally there are some benefits: Your anger may unearth an unspoken truth, bringing the integrity of the situation *up* a notch. Or on rare occasions the other person may "blow" at the exact same time you do and then "come down," magically, at the same time you do as well, in which case the two of you become "synched up" and can connect and approach one another from a fresh, new angle.

But *unconscious* venting (lashing out before you can stop yourself) can be rather violent and dangerous. It's like entrusting your growth to a wounded rogue Part about to explode, and then crossing your fingers that this explosion will somehow magically occur before anything gets broken or anyone gets too hurt in the process. Also, it can be addictive— trapping you in a cycle of repeating pressure and release—because the pressure is temporarily gone, but the wounds are not.

Conscious venting is about actively noticing the buildup of pressure on your overtaxed Parts, and designing a release for the system that offers a CONstructive, rather than DEstructive, way to bring that pressure down. The single biggest factor with constructive venting is aiming the vented energy at something inanimate. Slam a pillow on the bed. Close the windows in your car and scream at the top of your lungs. Open and close a cabinet door repeatedly with heavy force. You can explore all kinds of creative ways to release pressure that is not aimed at anyone. And instead of just doing so because "I can't stand this anymore," think about doing so *as a gift to your inner configuration.* Imagine the power of shaking off pressure for the specific purpose of caring about overtaxed Parts within you and recognizing they need some relief. Caring in this way can bring about a completely different feel to your attuning inward and attending to the buildup of pressure within.

4. Translate Peak Moments Into Something to Aim For

One of the more advanced ways of coaxing your inner configuration into a healthier formation is to learn to work in a new way with what I call "Peak" moments. Peak Moments are those rare moments where the world outside matches your world inside in the most delicious of ways. It's as if the Universe has suddenly, inexplicably, offered up serendipity all around you that is *in full alignment* with something equally joyful—a temporary but fabulous "super-healthy inner configuration"—among all your Parts. On the outside, this might look like you delivering a speech and nailing it, or feeling deep joy all throughout your body during a meaningful hug, or allowing peace to enter you in a quiet, mystical corner of the woods, or even just hitting a green light, ten stoplights in a row, and feeling increasingly blown away by the sheer serendipity of it. On the inside, in this exact same Peak Moment, whether you are conscious of it or not, *every one of your Parts* feels (momentarily) fully included and embraced. Any resistance to harmony drops gloriously away. Parts that know each other and Parts that don't all seem to magically unite together (*how? what just happened?*) in a configuration that feels and is *deeply embracing,* allowing for a joyful, unburdened, more "tapped-in" version of you than you might usually get to experience.

UNHEALTHY   HEALTHY   SUPER—HEALTHY PEAK

Peak Moments are, however, by their very nature, fleeting. The eleventh green light turns red. The speech is over and you are suddenly filled with doubts about how it was received. The sun sets in the woods and it gets dark and scary and hard to find your way out.

So many of us cling to retreating Peak Moments in ways that reinforce our smallness, our aloneness, and our wounds. Many of us experience the passing of such a moment as a sad little opportunity to dig ourselves in deeper with narratives of loss, disappointment, difficulty, victimhood, and fateful bad luck. "It figures," we say. "I was wondering when the other shoe was going to drop. Just when things were really starting to cook, it all falls apart again. I have all the proof I need. I just can't have what I really want. Moments like that never last."

Does any part of that sound familiar? Maybe not in the areas of your life that are flowing, but perhaps in the ones in which you feel wounded or stuck in some way? Do you recognize the sound of a little Part within you that's almost weirdly excited to discover more proof that good things can't last for you, and to verify that in the end, the wounded Parts in you are always going to be left wanting?

What if there is another way of viewing all of this? What if you were to shift your orientation toward something more expansive than just how disappointing it is that magical moments recede? What if you began to discover the gift not only of "having a serendipitous moment" but also the gift of "losing a serendipitous moment?"

If I were "The Universe" and I was trying to help sweet little you to wake up and start taking more ownership for navigating yourself forward in meaningful, feel-good ways, you know what I would do? I would make it possible for you to know that you are *capable of feeling amazing and tapped in* to all of the Parts within you at once—all of them lovingly hugging together and harmonious. I would present you with a moment where you could, through that magical (temporary) inner alignment, experience more of the energies flowing all around you (even the stoplight energies!). I would create an experience for you that would let you not just *hear* about such a possibility, or *observe* it in a friend, but *fully experience it for yourself*—in your body, with your emotions, in the way your thoughts might shift to a more promising vantage point during said magical moment. I would let you experience this fully, not just within the world but also *within your own experience and consciousness.*

And then, as "The Universe," you know what I would do next? When I was sure you had really felt it, that you were clear it was real—not a dream, not an imagining—I would remove it. Not because I am out to get you, or want to hurt you, but because this Universe is not about some genie in a bottle or angel in the sky dropping down to fulfill your every wish and do it all *for* you. This Universe is about the incredible journey *you are capable of making* when you know Who You Are, and how to navigate from the finest places within you—from within a Parts configuration that honors *every* Part within you—toward something specific and better.

So, as an advocate for you, I would want you to have a very solid TASTE of what it feels like to *be in alignment*, inside (with Parts) and outside (with the energies of the Universe). And then I would want for you, wish for you, cheer on the sidelines for you, to use that knowledge of what it's possible for you to feel, to start navigating forward, *creating your own experience of such alignment within yourself.*

The experience of "Parts magically aligning" every once in a while has to be *present* for you to understand how powerful such a thing is, and how good it feels. That said, it also has to be *absent* in order for you to feel the truth of your current configuration "default setting," and for you to develop the *desire*—hunger even—to navigate toward wholeness and peace, in your own way, using your own powers, creating your own unique life.

The invitation here is to start seeing all the Peak Moments you've already had as a kind of "photo album" of how it's possible for you to feel—a photo album you can sit down and share with the Parts within you, saying, "This is what we're shooting for. This is the feeling and the configuration we want. Do you see it? Do you remember how that felt? Who needs what, inside of me, for us all to collectively be able to create more of that, more of the time?"

This, more than anything else, sets the stage, beautifully, for true healing.

5. Heal Wounded Parts

By far the most powerful and lasting way to strengthen your inner configuration (and the approach we will spend the most time with) is to learn to "talk to yourself"—or, perhaps said better, to talk *with* yourself: to foster connective relationships among you and your Parts through inspired, loving, and purposeful dialogue. It can be very simple if you let it: Life is all about the places inside you that hurt, and your ability to *meet* yourself there. And life is also all about the places inside you that are gloriously strong and clear beyond your imagining, and your ability to access them more fully, when the hurts are more fully healed.

What's needed, especially for hurting or wounded Parts within you, is love, curiosity, and attunement shined inward, in the exact places where it was missing, way back when, when these Parts got damaged and solidified into alienated, isolated "beings."

The orientation toward healing wounded Parts within you is so powerful and the impact can be so transforming and profound that this idea deserves a chapter all its own. Read on and discover how, in Ceremonial Time, *to become, for wounded Parts, the loving presence they have lacked until now.*

Chapter 17

Healing Wounded Parts

One of the most powerful teachings I learned at the University of Santa Monica was the very simple concept that:

> ## "Healing is the application of loving to the places inside that hurt."

This idea begins with allowing hurting Parts to *be heard* (by you). And, as a result of being heard, to *be healed*.

What I am talking about is NOT seeking out a healer (though there are many on the planet who are talented), NOT relying on a psychic (though many of them really do know things), NOT even tracking down a guru (though I have had a few myself and having them has been wonderful).

What I am talking about is stepping into the full potential of this particular life-altering concept: *You have within you everything you need to heal yourself.*

It's an inner-power-awakening idea. In my experience, people who walk the planet understanding this tend to *look different*, physically *and* energetically. And being in their presence *feels* different. They're generally less fearful, less needy, relying less on what happens around them to determine their well-being or signal disruptions within them. People who know this about themselves tend to be more internally peaceful, internally curious, and internally creative beings.

And embedded within this idea is an even *deeper* truth. It's a revelation, really:

There is no one on the planet who is more perfectly calibrated to heal the wounds in you than YOU.

You are the only one in this entire world who has been *present* for the formation of every single trauma, wound, or slight that you have experienced. I get that what I am saying is obvious, on one level. But it is truly *radical*, on another: YOU are the most perfectly equipped healer for the wounds in YOU. And I also get that we might need to back up a step or two to really bring this into the light where you can not only make sense of the idea but also work with it, practically, in ways that can allow you to heal and grow.

It all starts with a simple inner dialogue of the most basic, gentle, nature. It's a dialogue between you and a Part within you that has been wounded in some way. Such a dialogue is available to you anytime. It can help a lot, I find, to follow four basic steps:

- **A. Scan the Field**
- **B. Listen In**
- **C. Exercise Your Capacity to "Hold"**
- **D. Respond from a YES Orientation**

An Introduction to Heading Inward

What I am about to describe to you is strange, because it involves the nuts and bolts of "talking to yourself" on a level you may never have engaged in before. But when you get right down to it, it's probably no stranger than any of the occasional serendipitous moments you've had that seem larger than life or that exist "outside of time." And, in fact, many of you, when you stop to notice it, can hear faint little dialogues playing inside of you all the time anyway.

That said, I want to teach you what no one taught me—what I found my way into, through spending my adult years focusing on stuckness and flow. I learned, in essence, that locating and talking to "places within yourself" is infinitely more do-able *if you dare to suspend doubt and simply believe, even just briefly, that there really are Parts inside of you,* and that they have the ability to converse with you. A lot is possible in the moment you decide to "know" that Parts are there. You need only to be polite yet clear in letting those Parts know that you are sincere about wanting to connect with them.

The magical ingredient to dialoguing with Parts within you is your willingness to imagine that such a thing is possible.

A. Scanning the Field: Calling All Parts

Scanning the Field means making it known to "everyone in there" that you are present and ready to dialogue in a newly conscious way. It might sound something like this:

> *Attention Every Part, Aspect, or*
> *Collection of Energy Within Me:*
> *I am calling out to you. I don't know yet where you are, exactly, or what you are. I don't know what you need or what you have to offer, or how I can help you or receive from you. But I am interested in learning these things. I am inviting you, in this very moment, to rise up within my awareness so that we can make an official "first contact." And I am setting an intention for this to happen in a manner that represents a shift, and a stretch that is healthy, safe, manageable, connective, and loving. I am not asking for anything that any Part isn't ready for. I am simply opening my heart and my mind, and inviting you to do the same. I am making a space within myself for us to gather together here to learn what is possible.*

Basically, you're calling a meeting. You're assuming that you have the power to do so, and trusting that there will be a response within you that you can detect and begin to connect with.

For most of you, this will work best when you are alone. It often helps to do something ceremonial—light a candle, take a deep breath, or play a certain piece of music that resonates with you. It helps to do anything at all that signifies to you that you are *up to something different, in the name of love.* You might say the words above, out loud. You might choose your own words. For some of you, doing this once will be enough to make full and surprising contact. For others, your consciousness may need several connection-rehearsals, or you may need to try it in the presence of an "energetically comfortable" friend who perhaps has some experience or comfort conversing with voices within themselves. But for any of you who want to make this connection, it is my experience that if you stay with it, it will come.

INITIATING A DIALOGUE

Twenty years ago I met the man who was to become the husband I would go the distance with. He quickly became and has remained the love of my life: a caring partner who sees me for who I am and who regularly makes it fertile and inviting for me to grow and evolve. I connected with him soon after my divorce was final—too soon, many feared. But we don't necessarily get to choose how fast or slow our newly clarified wishes manifest. And one day, very shortly after my travels around the country and my divorce, there he was.

For one sweet and magical year we deepened and expanded in the presence of one another, carefully at first, and then with more confidence and certainty. At the end of that year, we both felt the tug to become engaged. We planned that at exactly 2 a.m., we would meet atop a giant train trestle out in the cornfields of Ohio—the very spot where we had spent our first date together—to make it official.

Meeting at 2 a.m. meant that I had hours and hours that evening all to myself to use however I wanted. I knew next to nothing about Parts at the time. I did know in some general way that all signs seemed to point toward building a life with this gentle, authentic, and adventurous man. Yet I also knew that things had felt "all systems go" for me once before in the marriage department and that, nonetheless, I had left that experience feeling chewed up, spit out, and not entirely clear what, exactly, had caused things to run so far off the rails.

I knew enough to know that while it LOOKED like the problem was "out there" with "that last guy," there was much more to it, and the "much more" seemed to have to do with my own relationship with myself— my own ability to hear not just the voices cheering me onward in the foreground, but also the other Parts, hiding, fearful of speaking up, and possibly having something important to say to me as well.

At 7:00 that muggy summer night, I sat in my little apartment bedroom on the floor next to a full-length mirror. I looked into that face of mine, to see what I could see. Without knowing exactly what I was doing, I called my first "meeting." I leaned forward and stared right into my own eyes until what I saw blurred and shifted and didn't even really look like me anymore. And I said these words:

> *Hello in there. It's me. As most of you know, I am about to step over a line and into the world of joining my life with someone else. But I want to be very clear with all of you, whoever you are, that I have not stepped over that line yet. And while I really want to, and feel ready to, and feel rightful about it, I want to learn how to check in more deeply with all of you. I want to make it safe for you to share with me what you see, what you think, what I might be missing. I want your collective advice on navigating this. What do I not know? Who's in there? Is anyone scared? Does anyone see dangers I don't see? Can you help me? Do you trust me? Do you know how much I genuinely want to hear you, even though I might be afraid of what you have to say? I can't promise I will do every single thing every one of you asks me to do, but I can tell you it is my intention to listen with a full and open heart and to hear you. I want to hear you. I realize in this moment that is truly, truly what I want. Can you hear me? Who needs me to know what?*

What followed was a cacophony of voices. Not "voices" like the way you might hear the sound of humans in the next room at a party. But voices like the way you "hear" voices during a dream. It was a strange blur of excitement, as if the many proponents of this marriage were desperately trying to be sure to *talk over everyone else.* I also had the sense that some Parts were not strong enough or practiced enough to fight their way to the forefront of all this, but really did have something to say—which I discovered I was interested in, and also terrified of hearing. A very Logistical thought shot through my mind: *Maybe it's too late to be asking this. I have a date to get engaged in seven hours. Am I really in a position to handle finding out I am not supposed to do this?*

147

But to my everlasting benefit, I was able to let go of that line of thought. It felt like a Herculean effort, in some strange deep inner way, to tune inward and *not have an agenda* about whether I was, in fact, going to get engaged this night or not. It felt sort of like *p-u-l-l-l-i-n-g* off some tightly adhered outer shell of Logistical Attunement. The shell felt sort of rigid in some imaginary way, and not easy to free myself from. But I was firm and focused, and I did it. And in so doing, I learned that that is exactly how we truly *Enter In.* We leave the Logistical World behind as completely as possible, and with it, we leave behind all our agendas and ideas about how things are "supposed to go." And then we listen.

I think maybe I'm going to need to hear from you one at a time, I said, into the general inner melee. *I literally do have all night. Do you have the ability to arrange yourselves? Can I ask each one of you, however many there are, one after the other, if I might have your blessing to go forward into this engagement?*

Well, strange as it sounds, they really did take turns. All I did was ask, and it happened. They told me all kinds of things. (You can try this yourself now, or any time. Or you can read on, to learn more of the larger picture before you turn inward.)

B. Listening In

I ended up being in front of that mirror for two *hours.* It took a strange kind of attunement and concentration that I was not used to tapping into. There were tears. Moments of profound excitement. I learned really strange things. And all because I had decided it might be possible to have such a conversation, *and it was.*

There were Parts that had a facility with jumping to the forefront. They went first—showing me all the ways that this particular man was amazing, wise, loving, and rightful. It felt good and affirming to hear.

In the aftermath of that, there were Parts that had questions for me. Had I thought about my hopes for the two of us five years out? Ten? Fifty? Did it look anything like what *he* was hoping for? Or this: Could I identify moments in the past year where I had missed opportunities to really hear him as he was attempting to share deeper things with me? How might I work with this, learning to become more attuned to him over time?, they wanted to know. And how might I learn to do this in ways that deepened rather than compromised my own attunement to myself? These were really interesting questions that "I would not have thought of on my own." Or so it seemed. They were new, non-scary lines of thought that felt good, and helpful, and hopeful.

But most fascinating of all were the Parts that came forward, eventually, after everyone else, to show me the places where I was still wounded. These Parts showed me, sort of verbally, sort of with a strange kind of imagery, how being around someone wonderful, who is a good fit, in the early stages of love, can be fantastic, not just because it feels so good, but because it can provide some relief from wounds. They showed me how great it is to get that relief and also how that level of relief is not the same as—and should not be confused with—truly healing a wound. They opened up to me. They cried. They keened. It was very intense to see this level of hurt existing within myself.

They were afraid that I might be confusing early love (beautiful love, strong-fit love, great-potential-for-growth love) with having healed the places inside of me that were hurting. And they expressed a concern that if I misunderstood or lost track of the places inside that still needed my attention—an attention which could not be delivered through another, no matter how much that other loved me—then I might be setting myself up for a kind of confusion about what I had with this man, and what our connection could and could not provide me.

This was pretty astonishing information. These were wounded Parts. Speaking. They were saying incredibly wise things. But they were also a mess—broken, sobbing, and truly upset. They weren't saying, "Thanks for hearing me this one time—now I am healed and feel fine." They were saying, "We need more. Don't abandon us. Our work has just begun."

Hmmm. What on earth had I tapped into? And yet, it was exactly what I had asked for, and never would have been able to hear if I had not (a) been willing to believe such a dialogue was possible and (b) set aside my own agenda (*just tell me I can marry him!*) and dared to truly listen.

In fact, no one within me—even those wounded, sobbing Parts—said that I should not marry this man. This simple truth felt simultaneously like an amazing relief and a powerful endorsement—a Deeper YES. It occurred to me that there was a world of difference between going forward *hoping* I had inner endorsement as opposed to deeply *knowing*

I had it. I had taken the time to find out and now I really knew. What power, strength, and courage that gave me, and has given me, all the many years of this marriage—just the simple experience of *asking* inward, as opposed to "telling" inward.

One big thing I learned on that day was how little I had tended to tune in to the hurting places inside of me until that night. What I have come to know about wounded Parts, resting further back in our psyches, is that if they are given an audience, and checked in with every once in a while, they pretty quickly become wise and helpful, which is a pretty amazing thing if you stop and think about it.

Our most wounded Parts hold within them the seeds for great clarity and growth.

Conversely, as I have seen over and over again with clients (and, if I am perfectly honest, with myself, even now, sometimes), if we choose to ignore those places—those Parts within us that are hurting or damaged— they do lie low and tuck away. But when the pressure builds to a certain tipping point, there is literally an explosion. They become LOUD PARTS. They move to the forefront in ways that are not team-player-like at all. They become overwhelmed with the pressure of an unhealed past hurtful experience and they take over for a while as Rogue Parts and often wreak havoc.

The simple fact that I started to address the Parts within me as a group began to *change something within me.* I started operating, in that strange Ceremonial Time, as if it were possible to talk to all Parts at once. Which means I was addressing Parts that perhaps until that moment had not been aware they were part of a group at all.

In the strange energies of the inner world, *how we are with the issue IS the issue.* If the way we are with our inner configuration is oblivious that it is there, then we never look at it, work with it, or invite it to evolve from a "busy city street" of strangers into a well-attuned circle of intimates that work as teammates. If the way we are with Parts in isolation is that we ignore them, then they remain estranged and we remain at the mercy of their strange pressure-driven antics. If the way we are with the whole lot of them is *addressing them as if they are a team with the power to organize and work together for the highest good of all concerned*, well, lo and behold! Our attunement and loving attention can invite and encourage re-configuration to happen.

And peeking around with curiosity is just the beginning! The real change happens when we not only set the stage and listen, but when we also respond in ways that invite the conversation to elevate to the next level. That's when inner dialogues and, correspondingly, life in the world "out there" can become really exciting and uplifting. And it can't really happen unless we have developed our capacity to "hold" the energy of a difficult Part *before we respond*.

C. Exercising Your Capacity to "Hold"

I was incredibly lucky that night in front of the mirror because the hurting Parts inside showed up so straightforwardly. They were so grateful to be acknowledged, so ready to speak up, and so clear in what they had to say. I had done a lot of inner work at my grad school, and I think it showed in the way those hurting Parts seemed to trust me and speak freely.

It is not always so.

Many times I have helped a client to get into dialogue with an upset Part, only to find that the Part in question feels forgotten, is utterly furious, and has a lot to say that is ugly and hard to hear. It's important to be able to stay present and conscious when this happens, and to be able to make it safe for an upset Part to "say its piece." For this reason, over time, my mirror approach has evolved, along with my coaching practice, to an office setup of two empty chairs designed to facilitate conversations with Parts, many of which first appear in an upset state. Inspired by the work of the founder of Gestalt therapy, Fritz Perls, one chair is for a client to put "themselves" in, and the second chair, directly facing it just a few feet away, holds a space for a Part (hurting or otherwise) to sit and speak when that Part feels ready.

To create the strongest arrangement for a healthy dialogue, I invite the client to start in "their" chair, but then to physically move back and forth between the two chairs each time they give voice to one side of the conversation or the other. In short, they "embody" each side of the conversation fully. In this way, a Part that has never had true, official "real-world air time" before gets a voice *and* an "audience."

The way you listen, as an audience, to your own upset Part, *matters deeply*.

I very specifically invite clients, to the full extent that they are able, to listen to a Part—even a ferociously angry one—in a manner that invites the Part to open up and share as much as it is willing and able to. The idea is to make it feel *possible* for that Part to voice a potentially difficult message: about pain, about misunderstanding, about disappointment, and about all the anger and bile that can get generated when that Part's narratives start to initially come forward.

Whether I am assisting another or just teeing up my own inner dialogues, I do everything in my power to create an environment that will feel and *be* safe for a Part to speak freely. I do a verbal setup, inviting everyone to breathe deeply, clarifying "who" is in each chair and what our intention is in setting up such a conversation. I invite silence for several minutes before the dialogue begins, to allow it to start up in its own natural way. I issue a verbal invitation to this Part to come forward and to speak or not speak *as it sees fit*. I invite the conversation to play out in a manner that is "for the highest good of all concerned." Before we even dive in, I offer the option of future conversations if everything doesn't fall fully into place in this one, to relieve the pressure and to help establish the foundation for an ongoing relationship. I do all of these things for others not because my presence is a necessary ingredient to the conversation but as a model for my client. It is our shared hope that he or she will feel inspired to take ownership for initiating these stage-setting steps going forward. And that soon, the client, and their Parts, will not need me there at all in order to dive in and create full, beautiful, ongoing dialogues together. As you and I move together through the elements of setting up such a dialogue, I offer the same hope and wish for you, because I believe you are capable of this. I think everyone is, if only they will try, and believe.

Far more important to the healing power of the conversation that ensues than *anything* in the setup, though, is the fundamental importance of genuine, inviting energy flowing from the "self" chair to the "Part" chair. I encourage my client to stay open, in listening mode, and to release any knee-jerk urge to judge or to try to steer the conversation.

The healing potential of a Parts Conversation is directly correlated to your capacity to remain fully curious, free from the compulsion to judge.

This kind of stance can be challenging out in the "real world," because we can bump up hard against unyielding issues and wounds in others. But for some very important reasons, this is not the case *at all* with Parts conversations. In my now extensive experience in working with my own inner configuration, and helping with that of countless others, I have come to know this: *Any Part that knows your intention is to listen with an open heart will offer up as many tries as necessary until a true connection is made.*

Why? Because the deepest desire of every disenfranchised Part is completely harmonious with the deepest desire of anyone who is ready to heal:

RE-CONNECTION.

When we *enter into an inner dialogue with re-connection at the center of our heart*—no matter how broken a Part may feel or how unpracticed we may be at listening without judgment—*unforeseen, powerful, wisdom-cracking, light-filled conversations can begin to occur.* I have seen it over and over again, within myself and among a wide range of others.

Better still, once non-judgmental, curious healing conversations of this nature start happening, they don't stop. They start up more and more frequently, more and more spontaneously. They move beyond one conversation with one Part and start to burst forth in other newly ready places all throughout your inner Parts configuration. And before you know it, they begin to play out in the "real world" as well—in the dialogues you find yourself in with friends, in the dialogues you find yourself in with Nature, in the dialogue you find yourself in *with the Essence Level itself.* Healthy conversations tend to breed more healthy conversations.

This is true if the conversation is simple and easy, like my mirror-talk the night of my engagement. And it is equally true even if the conversation begins with a Part that wants to scream or cry, rage or blame, simmer or whimper. It is true even if it all starts with you sitting in the listening chair longing to cover your ears, to turn away, to cry, or to yell something reactive and terrible back to a very upset Part.

It is true because in the *moment* we call forward such a conversation within ourselves—one that says, *I am here; I want to know you; I want to understand what I am missing*—we have PIVOTED in the direction of healing.

It can be scary. Upsetting. Weird. Embarrassing. A Part's need to rant or cry can appear, at first, bottomless. We are seeing, in essence, the pain from something that happened to us long before and has remained unhealed, on some significant and lasting level. We are seeing that pain through the lens of the Part that "took the hit" and is in some ways, deep inside of us, still taking it. We are seeing that pain or confusion or overwhelm in its purest form, isolated down to one "character" Part living in pain, hidden inside us. It's a lot to take in.

But this is a real moment of truth. How we respond to this Part in this moment has a lot to do with how profoundly healing can take place.

D. Responding from a YES Orientation

Who among us does not want, deeply, at our most core level, to simply be who we are, without editing, without hiding, without constricting? And how good and amazing does it feel, ultimately, when we allow that?

Allowing it for some of us is more common; for others of us, more rare. But when any of us experiences a moment of truly being and expressing Who We Really Are, we relax, we breathe more deeply. We begin to hear ourselves more clearly.

Such is the case with wounded Parts. When we are capable of simply holding a space that is large enough for them to say whatever they have to say, to cry or rage about whatever they have to cry or rage about, there starts to come an end to it, a possibility for it to reach its logical conclusion and then, finally, to transform into something truer, less constricted: a more mature and authentic—healed—expression.

I can't tell you how many times I have watched someone give full voice to a wounded Part—ranting, raving, crying, blaming, filled with anger or shame or any number of difficult energies, only to have that Part *transform before our eyes once it finally gets to speak and feel heard.*

Anger turns slowly to tears. Tears turn to longer silences and deeper breaths. Deep breaths expand into increasingly graceful inner spaces, eyebrows starting to rise, a new thought beginning to form: awareness and insight blowing through like a fresh, cool breeze in a formerly airless space. New questions start to arise from within. Love and peace can and do fill the spaces that have been newly cleared and expanded.

In the "real world," blowups play out in lots of fractured ways. One person can push too hard, or retreat too quickly, and cause the other person to pull away. The connection gets broken.

But in Ceremonial Time, in a world deep within our own selves, in relation to all of our Parts, no matter how far one Part pulls away, there is nowhere, really, to go that is outside of the system.

If you are patient and present and can hold a space; if deep in your heart you are ready to *make the re-connection,* then a re-connection *will* happen, because it is the most basic shared desire of you and all your Parts.

When it comes to healing, the love you breathe into your response to any Part that has finally, bravely, spoken its piece (or even a *piece* of its piece, as healing sometimes happens all at once and sometimes happens over multiple important conversations) is your grandest opportunity.

A YES ORIENTATION TO LOVING

How you respond—the attuned or judging way you acknowledge a hurt inside you—determines your answer to one of the most profound questions that lies at the heart of each one of us who has suffered any kind of hurt, exclusion, or trauma, at any point in our lives.

QUESTION: Is it time, now, for the disenfranchised, abandoned, forgotten, left-behind Parts within me to re-connect?

Try asking yourself, and see what you get for an answer, because:

In the moment that

YES

becomes your orientation
toward a hurting Part,
the healing process
comes alive within you.

At the very Essence-filled center of Who You Are:
All Parts belong.
All Parts are loved.
All Parts have a rightful place in your inner configuration and deserve to find and express that rightfulness.

We are not *really* in dialogue until we, from a place of truly hearing the voices within us, respond to them from within our own ability to love.

The good news is that anything you say—to any Part within you—that communicates *YES, I want to help you say your piece*—will bring about healing.

YES.
Yes, it is okay that you are hurting.
Yes, it makes sense.
Yes, I am here for you.
Yes, I really do want to hear.
Yes, even, to your pain—there is room for it to express itself here; you have nothing to hide.
No more "no" to your presence, your pain, your secrets, your abandonment.
YES to you.
YES to all of us.

If you aren't sure how to do that, you don't have to flounder. You just have to read on.

Chapter 18

Connecting with Your Higher Self

Once you have responded with a YES orientation—once you practice voicing authentic acceptance toward ALL the Parts within yourself—roadblocks and resistances truly do melt away, new solutions and arrangements from within begin to rise, and your life can become filled with more inner spaciousness, ease, and flow.

But if this is starting to sound a little too much like an oversimplified, "Why can't everybody in there just get along?" then let's look a little closer. Because I get that it's one thing to say, "Just have a YES orientation to all your Parts." It may be another thing entirely to enact this from an authentic place within you. If you tend to be reactive when someone spits bile or blame at you in the "real world," how are you supposed to suddenly be a master of YES orientation when you are dealing with a nasty Rogue Part on the inside?

UPSET PARTS ARE EASIER THAN UPSET PEOPLE

Well, one thing that helps is that upset Parts are generally so overblown in their upset, once they are genuinely given the floor, they have more in common with a two-year-old having a tantrum than with a savvy colleague making a subtle, unnerving dig. Two-year-olds may be annoying from time to time, but it's rare that one of their meltdowns will sway *you* to believe the world is ending, too, or to lose your own bearing while they lose theirs. For another, unlike foes in the real world who "stick to their unhealed guns," upset Parts generally morph right before your eyes when they are given even a modicum of love. It's a truly amazing thing to be present for, and it is REAL! I see it with clients—and with myself—any time an upset individual is given some Parts-oriented breathing room. When you bump into someone else's wounds in the form of bad behavior in the "real world," those wounds could be "up" for any number of reasons—many of them closer to venting than healing. But when you consciously invite an upset Part to say its piece, it's usually pretty clear that whatever antics are taking place in the initial conversation are *in the name of getting things up to the surface for healing.* You can relax into the knowledge that any invited Part that has stepped forward is doing so because *healing is available.* If it starts with a tantrum, so be it. That's just where it *starts.* Healing is where it is headed if you conscientiously invite it.

But there's one thing that matters more than all of these reassurances put together, and it's this: There is a hard way and an easy way to offer up a loving, accepting YES orientation to an upset Part.

The hard way is *struggling* to come off as a centered version of yourself. The hard way "takes everything you've got" and still might not be enough. With the hard way, having a "YES" orientation to an upset Part behaving badly can leave you feeling like a parent, enraged at your child, popping every vein in your neck in order to subdue your own anger while trying to appear unaffected in the eyes of your errant, triggering child. The hard way is based on the belief that "you don't have it in you" to be amazing in the presence of a venting Part, so the closest you can get is to pretend that you do.

But here's the thing: In fact, you *do* have it in you to be that amazing. Perhaps not every place inside of you is currently that amazing, but one place always is.

A MAGICAL PLACE WITHIN YOU

There is a very specific, Essence-oriented location within you, and when you are operating from within that place, being amazing is natural, rightful, easy, and deeply impactful.

This is a crazy-powerful idea, so hold on tight: If you can imagine that there are Parts inside of you that are a concentration of distressed, overwhelmed, or hurting energies, is it so much of a stretch to imagine that there is a specific location inside of you where your finest and truest energies intersect and come vibrantly, brilliantly alive? Is it so much of a stretch to imagine that if you embrace this idea and focus your consciousness on this area, your connection with it will deepen, broaden, and expand into something marvelous that *feels better?*

Where is that place?, you likely want to know. *Is that place a Part, too?*

Well, no. That place is not a Part. But it is an important and very real energetic "location."

I like to think of it as **The Finest, Truest Place Within You.**

You can call it anything you like: your Higher Self, your Core Essence, your Authentic Innermost Voice. It's that luminous, resplendent flow of energies moving through you, fed by the deep life force of this planet and extending out toward the wonder of all the cosmos. Sometimes it plays out as a trickle within you, and other times it is a radiant, bountiful flow. But it is always, always present. And the choice to engage with it, and expand your access to it, is always yours.

The availability of that flow—and the freedom with which it can move— is directly correlated with how ready you are, right now, in your own consciousness, to simply know this:

Essence energy
is alive within you.

The more you orient your consciousness toward this, the more beautiful your life can become. The more you forget this, or fight against the YES of this, the more challenging your experience becomes.

We looked in Section 1 at what it would take for you to wake up to the wonder of the Essence energy all around you. I have alluded to the fact that such energy is *in* you as well. But now is the moment where we invite that idea to shift from an entertaining theory and a remote possibility to an actual place within you that you can learn to operate from more and more of the time. Because that place is there! And because, really, why *wouldn't* you, if you could?!

And ... you can. Essence energy *is* alive inside you.

Close your eyes for even just a sliver of a second, daring to know that this is true (yep, right now), and you can feel it: a little shiver. A flutter of inner awareness. A place in the background of your consciousness shifting just a little more forward in alignment with your purposeful, exploratory attention.

Why not invite much, much more of that?

Connecting with the wonder of your Finest, Truest Self doesn't have to be just "an idea you like that might help." It can be *The Way You Joyfully Live Life*. These three steps can assist you in doing exactly that:

Step 1: Ask for Your Higher Self
Step 2: Pull Things Apart
Step 3: Put Things Back Together

Let's look at them one at a time over the next few chapters.

Step 1: Ask for Your Higher Self

You have, within you, in the exact location I am referring to, a "Higher Self." It's always there, just as the Essence Level all around you is always there, whether you know it or not.

Losing touch with this Higher Self makes you fragile.

Being in ongoing connection with it makes you ... *you.* When you are in touch with your Higher Self, you get to be the version of you that is unhindered by others' dramas and strengthened by understanding your own. And, because of that, you get to be far more vibrant, curious, adventurous, and *free*.

You may think that "conjuring" this voice is hard to do. And I am here to tell you, having seen individuals who are new to it do this over and over again in my work, that it is simultaneously incredibly hard AND unbelievably easy.

Here's what's hard: You have to actually do it.

You can't think about it, or "sort of" do it, or enter into it the way you might go to a psychic and try to "trip her up" and prove she can't really see things. You have to use a muscle you may not often use. It's the muscle of *not doing anything else* except tuning in to your Highest Self.

It's hard because we live in a culture that does not reinforce doing this. It's hard because you will "forget" to do it, even though it helps. It's hard because even when you remember to do it, you may find yourself pleading and begging with your Higher Self to say what you want it to say, which is a completely different dynamic than daring to really listen. Odd, eh? Making all the arrangements to put yourself in the presence of your own greatness and then trying to argue it into some other more seemingly convenient shape. But it happens, more than you might guess, even by those of us who get far enough into our own potential to have a direct and somewhat regular audience with our Higher Self.

LISTENING IN PLACE OF PLEADING

When I was pregnant with my first baby, I began to awaken to what a profound transformation was playing out right under my nose (quite literally). My life-coaching practice at the time involved significant local travel and frequent, intense three-hour sessions. I had no idea what the final month of my pregnancy would bring in terms of energy flow, but I began to sense myself slowing down and pulling in a bit as the birth month drew near. I didn't want to deliver a crappy product to my clients, nor did I want to push myself past the point of well-being in the process of helping others. So I asked my Higher Self for some clarity around whether or not I should work in the ninth month. To my delight, I got a rather immediate and clear response:

> Tell all your clients you will come to their home for a three-hour session as planned in that last month, but that, at the end of one hour, you will excuse yourself to sit alone in their bathroom and ask if you have "high clearance" to continue. Don't come out until you are certain you have received an answer. If you get clearance, the session can continue. If not, refund them for the two unused hours, go home, and take a nap.

Hmmm. This felt a bit "out there," professionally, to me. I had let all my clients know that I had no idea, once this baby was born, when or if I would return to work. So for everyone, myself included, these were potentially final sessions, which might be getting cut unexpectedly short at the very last second. Even so, I was "fluent" enough by then to assume this internal voice guiding me was worth trusting. For that reason, I confidently shared my new directive with my clients, all of whom were willing to proceed this way.

When the ninth month came, I stuck to the agreement, set a little timer, and in each session crawled off into my client's bathroom after the first hour. Perched there, fully clothed upon their toilets, I would silently call inward to my Higher Self on the subject of clearance.

But did I quiet myself first? Release all attachment to the outcome? Orient myself toward listening? I did not. As unlikely as this sounds, I sat there all dressed up, on someone else's toilet, during someone else's billable time, pleading. Session after session I found myself putting all my energy into making a case to my Higher Self about the verdict I wanted it to come up with:

> *Listen, here's the thing. This client and I are covering a lot of ground here. We're really on a roll. This might be the last time I ever see this person. This session just wouldn't feel complete if we stopped right now. I get that you said we might have to cut it short, but could we not? I could nap right after the three hours are over! How about that? Please? I mean, think about it. I think that would take care of anything critical. You see where I am going with this, right? I feel like I can keep going. I seriously do. Please?*

Everything within me fought against simply tuning in. I sounded like a child begging a parent. Even though I thought of myself as a relatively evolved being with pretty easy access to my Higher Self, here I was, huddled over a commode, internally stage-whispering and fighting with all my might against listening to whatever inner wisdom I might have to dispense.

It is this tendency within us to want to "make it how we want it" that can make tuning in seem hard. We get so afraid of what our Higher Self *might* say that we create scenarios where we talk instead of listen. I do, anyway. You might, too. We have to learn to wake up to what is possible within us. And we have to dare to quiet down and listen.

Tick, tick. The clock is ticking. My client is out there waiting. And I am pleading away with my Higher Self—something I would never advise any client to do.

During the entirety of the time I was pleading, I had no ability whatsoever to actually *hear* my Higher Self. Higher Selves, I find, are eternally patient. And they very, very rarely interrupt or cut us off. They let us do our thing. They are amazing when we give them the floor. But when we don't, we are cut off from them—not because of THEM, but because of US.

So there's me, chattering away, trying hard to—what?—*manipulate the wisest place within me?!* And all I'm getting back is silence. Not stony silence. Not like my Higher Self is a great big baby and is stonewalling me. Just the kind of silence I get when my phone is hung up. There is not a connection, so there is nothing there to hear.

The effort it took me, over and over again, in those various bathrooms, to shift out of that frantic, pleading, manipulative mode (that was a Part talking, I now know!) and into the deep breath of acceptance was immense. It was like moving a boulder within me. It was "hard," in some strange, non-Logistical way.

But I did it. Eventually, I always did it.

You can do it, too. And I will help you.

I *always* got an answer when I finally shifted gears in those bathrooms. It came forward easily and clear as a bell.

About one in ten times I got this: *It's time to go home now, sweetheart.*

Just like that. Kind. Attuned. Simple. Always, in the moment it happened, I knew that this caring edict was a rightful one. I could feel a place inside of me—a place that had been trying and pushing so hard—almost burst into tears with relief. Again: a Part, I now know.

And instead of being embarrassed when I went back out to my client to deliver the verdict, I felt clear, centered, kind, and ready to exit. I knew I had prepared for this possibility well, in a way that was respectful of them *and* me. I also felt that what I was doing, in leaving, was truly valuable. It was a very attuned, higher-court judgment call on how my energies could best serve the planet right then. I really needed to go home. It was time to lie down and put the finishing touches on building someone's *brain*—someone who would one day rise up and create passionate gifts of his own for this beautiful planet. Things were back in perspective, back in alignment internally, and I could move forward, *feeling endorsed in my choices from within*. Ah, what a remarkable feeling that is.

About thirty percent of the time, I would get specific and odd little directives from my Higher Self: *Go out there and ask Celia if she's willing to make you a peanut butter sandwich. If she is, we'll have the nutrients we need, and we can keep building while you work.*

Just as simple as that. I would go out there and ask. Celia (or whoever) would have some peanut butter on hand; I would eat it and feel better. And on we would go with our completion session.

About sixty percent of the time, though, after all that begging and wheedling, the answer I would get would be a full ringing endorsement to proceed: *You're all clear to stay and finish the session!*

What?

I wasted ten minutes of my client's time begging for this, and the answer was yes all along? Why couldn't that answer have just come forward the second I walked into the bathroom?

Why indeed.

Consider that there is a world of difference between begging, bargaining, cajoling—all versions of *tuning out* our Higher Self—and simply *tuning in.*

TUNING IN TO YOUR HIGHER SELF

Are you starting to be able to imagine, or even sense, that there are LOTS of voices inside you? That those voices that are unhealed will surely have their own (limited) understanding of *your* best interest and of the "larger picture?" Many of them have no real conception (yet) that there is more to "you" than just them, their hurt, and their wound-driven compulsions. But there is always one place inside of you that has the ability to see much farther in all directions, and sense what choices are for your highest good and for the highest good of all concerned. You can learn to attune to this voice and to distinguish it from the others. And you can learn to navigate the moments of your life, more and more, through its wisdom.

It happens when you stop talking, manipulating, and pleading with this place inside you that *can be trusted to help you,* once you let it. Once you, quite simply, "put it in the chair."

I have said that "conjuring" that Higher Self voice is hard, in a way, and it really is. *It's hard to let go of our desire to hear what we want to hear.* Sometimes when I look at people who can bench-press 300 pounds and I see the exertion on their face, I can relate. There's something oddly *strenuous* (for a split second anyway) about letting go of whatever I have been clinging to in my consciousness and *truly* opening to a more embracing, less controlling place within myself.

But once I have decided that I am all systems go, leaving my personal agenda behind me like an outgrown snake skin—the most *amazing things* happen with my Higher Self! And it takes no effort at all. It's the *deciding* that you are really going to engage with yourself on this level that takes a strange but very real kind of energetic "effort."

Once the decision is made, dialoguing with your Higher Self is one of the easiest, most surprising, most clarifying things you will ever do.

Ever heard yourself say something amazingly astute and think, "Where did *that* come from?" I watch clients have this experience *over and over again* when they dare to put their Higher Self in that second chair.

SURPRISING YOURSELF WITH YOUR OWN WISDOM

Ellen was a writer feeling stuck, trapped in her job, and frustrated. She was caught in repeating cycles and nervously watching her finances dwindle. Her efforts to shift gears frequently did not play out as she wished. But every single time we put her Higher Self in the chair, the things it said to her were so unexpectedly sensitive, uplifting, wise—right there in the middle of all her struggle and inner bedlam.

Each time she completed such a conversation (they are often fairly short—Ceremonial Time communications don't *take* a lot of "real time," interestingly), we would write down what her Higher Self had said, and marvel over it. It blew both of us away, not only because it was luminously insightful, but because it seemed so *perfectly calibrated to where she was and what she was ready to hear.*

Best of all, it seemed to take absolutely no effort for this perspective to come forward, *once the stage was set.* Sitting in the "Higher Self" chair, she would open her mouth and these illuminating re-framings would come exquisitely and fully present. It was beyond easy because it was so natural. But it was also hard. Meaning, despite these incredibly helpful revelations, each time I suggested we go to the chairs, Ellen, like so many of my clients, would groan and resist. And, like most of my clients, each time the short conversation had played itself out, she would comment on how beautifully the conversation had shifted in unforeseen ways, and how much lighter and more hopeful she felt.

I don't think it's unrelated to share that Ellen went on to write hundreds of prose poems, and that they are now published and available to all! When she does readings in public, people gasp. She has a unique and exceptional voice within her. We *all* do.

Setting yourself up for this *kind* of a conversation requires a deep inner shift, even if, in the Logistical world, it's as simple as laying out a couple of chairs and setting a clear intention.

There is always one voice—one place—within you that is evolved, tapped in, and ready to love you, now, just exactly as you are. Ready to shine light forward in celebration of your truest, highest path. Ask for that voice by whatever name you know it. Put yourself in one chair, put your Higher Self in the other, and experience the magic.

Chapter 19

Beautiful Conversations Within

What's great about gaining access to your Higher Self is that *so much more is possible.* The more you are in dialogue with your Higher Self, the more you find yourself operating from within a healthy, tapped-in place in your own consciousness. The exciting question becomes, *What shall I do with this newfound power and clarity?*

In the big picture, the options are limitless! Individuals tapped in on this level can and do make huge impacts for the good of those around them, and for the planet overall. But in the immediate moment, the more you can do to turn that Higher Self power inward and heal what is hurting inside of you, the more you will have to offer others. In the long run, having access to your Higher Self eases everything, but it doesn't automatically guarantee that the hurting places inside you will stop hurting. We talked about Step 1 as "asking for your Higher Self." But once you have done that, it's time to move on to Step 2 so that more clarity can be revealed.

Step 2: Pull Things Apart

When our lives get stuck, when we get overwhelmed, there is great power in separating out the pieces. Any time we separate out one *Part* of ourselves from "the rest of us" in conversation, we are doing something almost supernatural that is freeing in a way nothing else "on earth" really is.

When you put into one chair a Part of you that you've become aware is struggling, hurting, etc., and you put "yourself" in the second chair for a dialogue with that Part, guess who's in that second chair? It's you—all of you EXCEPT the Part of you that is hurting or upset.

167

Think about this for a moment.

It means that by "separating yourself out" into two "piles" of "you" for the purposes of this dialogue, you are giving yourself a stunning and powerful experience. In one chair, you're giving yourself a purified experience of the pain (free from the impulse to hide it or push it away). And in the other chair, *at the very same time*, you are giving yourself a purified experience of "you"—*you* getting to be exactly Who You Are ... except *without that pain.*

For the length of this Essence-Level dialogue, "you" are consciously *unblending* from the hurt, thanks to a conversational setup that makes the impossible (*I will never be free of this issue*) suddenly, instantaneously a reality (*Oh! Here I am. For this moment, anyway, free of this issue!*).

Under these very particular circumstances, for perhaps the first time in your adult life since this wound took hold, you can experience—not imagine, but actually *experience*—a new kind of freedom and a taste of what you will feel, in an ongoing way, when you are fully healed.

Any time you are in dialogue with a hurting Part, you are momentarily liberated from having to experience that pain as "you."

You are much closer to the Essence of Who You Are when you have separated out the "issue" and have put yourself in direct conversation with it.

This is such a profound idea: providing ourselves with opportunities to see who we would be if we were exactly Who We Are, except unencumbered by doubt, fear, resistance, pain, and the strange, small navigation patterns driven by the unhealed wounds within us.

It is strangely beautiful to sit in a room and watch a hurting Part get to finally cry, rage, or argue for its wounded view of the world. But the thing that blows my mind more than anything is the way in which such an activity allows whoever I am with to also sit in that *other* chair and experience what life is like when dealing *with* this troubled Part rather than dealing *as* this troubled Part, or from *within* this troubled Part.

The more you un-blend from the places inside that hurt, the clearer your access to your Higher Self.

If I had not seen it over and over and over again, I might doubt it. But I have seen it, and experienced it for myself. And now I want to show you how to do the same.

Step 3: Put Things Back Together

So: BOOM! This third step is where all the alchemy happens—where things can really change and really, *truly, deeply, lastingly* transform and heal.

Hurting parts have a sense of urgency *because* they are unhealed. This is fine because your biggest gift to this Part can be to simply offer it center stage with your attention and then really listen. How? You follow the energy toward increasingly meaningful, growth-oriented inner conversations—just as you might wish someone would do for you. And how do you do that? How do you become for this hurting Part exactly what it most needs? You begin by asking yourself:

How do I invite the inner conversations that are the most beautiful, healing, revelatory?

The most powerful, healing conversations happen when your most hurting Part is put in <u>direct dialogue</u> with your Higher Self.

BOOM!

When you put your Higher Self in one chair and your most hurting Part in the other, you bring the greatest concentration of your own love and clarity to the most hurting place inside you.

BOOM!

When you do this, a powerful healing connection gets made. Your most vulnerable self can bask in the warm glow of your most profound intuitive wisdom and love.

BOOM!

When you do this, time shifts, Ceremonially, into a unique kind of healing flow.

BOOM!

If there is a reason your spirit came to this planet, a purpose to your journey, that journey can engage in earnest once you "put things back together" *differently*—once you make the powerful connection between the most impoverished places within you and the most free-flowing and bountiful.

It sets something aright, to allow such a conversation—to, in Essence, no longer deny that you are—your Higher Self is!—powerful enough to hold a space for the most painful aspects of whatever aches inside you, so that it can be healed. You are—your hurting Parts are!—capable of coming forward from those hastily-slapped-together, cordoned-off corners within you, and into the fullness of your own light. And the fullness of your own inner light is full *enough*, tapped in *enough*, wise *enough*, to know exactly what to do with your unhealed Parts, when you put your Higher Self in a conscious, invited position to do so.

HIGHER SELF EMERGING

Never was this made so clear to me as when I did a session, years ago, with a client I'll call Katelyn. We bumbled upon her Higher Self voice in the most unlikely of ways: by putting her most troubled self in the chair and discovering we had landed on an inner gold mine. One day in a session, bemoaning her recent weight gain, Katelyn proclaimed, "I hate my body."

We decided to put her "Body" (troubled Part) in one chair and Katelyn herself ("the rest of me") in the other. Katelyn spoke to Body, complaining about how frustrating it was to watch and be part of this 60-year-old frame, packing on pounds. I sat there, taking in her anger and frustration, curious about what this troubled Part might have to say.

We were both utterly unprepared for what happened when Body spoke: Neutrality. Empathy. Curiosity. Deep understanding and appreciation for the frustration of the situation. Information: Body explained that no matter what food or drink was put into the system, it would process it, work to extract all available nutrients and release the toxins. It further explained that some foods were incredibly easy to work with, while others took great effort and were exhausting and depleting to the system. Even so, Body communicated an utter lack of judgment about what foods went in. Instead, Body lovingly communicated acceptance of what was challenging, and encouragement about what was possible—acceptance and encouragement to a degree that Katelyn had never before experienced, from "allies in the real world" or from anyplace within herself. Body's message culminated with a refrain that was to become the hallmark of all her Higher Self's future communications: a profound, lovingly calibrated steady stream of reminders that no matter what happened, Body (a true "embodiment" of her Higher Self) was there for Katelyn, a partner for life, ready to assist her in any endeavor, ready to love her no matter what she did, and ready to start afresh, in any moment Katelyn might choose, to physically move more; to turn more fully toward lighter, more freeing energies in the form of healthier foods. "Anything you want is possible for you and I am here to help you with it whenever you choose," Body said. "All you ever have to do is ask. I love you so much, Katelyn. I am fully here for you."

We found this Higher Self treasure trove inside Katelyn in the last place we ever might have thought to look for it, all because we were open to the possibility of an enlightening conversation and because we were willing to release any assumptions about what that conversation might "need to" look like. These days, when an issue is troubling Katelyn, she brings the related challenged Part into direct communion with Body. The healing has been profound. And the weight that so troubled her has come off!

Katelyn's inner life has shifted in powerful ways, as has her "real world" life. She walks lightly, has opened her heart in dialogue with others on brave new levels, to expansive and rewarding results. She has found an inspiring equilibrium inside her own body—discovering enthusiasm, energy, and excitement in eating lighter, healthier foods and also a newfound pleasure in deeply savoring the experience of an occasional, consciously chosen indulgence.

There is a freedom in her expression that surpasses anything she had access to within herself before she befriended her Higher Self, which, to this day, she refers to as "Body." She fulfilled a life dream, engaging in singing lessons with a renowned teacher. After dedicated hard work, she slid into a slender red taffeta gown before a packed room of $100-a-plate fans and performed a 20-song cabaret show, surprising not only the audience but herself with the way she had stepped forward so fully in this later chapter of her life to share her gifts, as music poured out of her.

Energy that used to get caught up in repeating stuck cycles within her now freely radiates outward, in the form of genuine and heartfelt expression. She is brave. She is beautiful, inside and out. And she has an inner loving voice guiding her.

When you "put things back together," offering unedited freedom-of-voice to troubled Parts, offering an open invitation for your Higher Self to step forward and meet yourself at the point of struggle, the dialogue of *you-with-you* can take powerful, unexpected, freeing, whimsical, self-supporting, and enlightening turns. Sometimes immediately, as in Katelyn's case. Sometimes after some pretty intense complaining, raging, crying, or general venting. But ultimately, if you stick with it, the voices of troubled Parts seem to transform into something more inclusive and expansive once they feel truly heard by the rest of YOU.

Why? Because you (and only you) are explicitly, perfectly, exactly calibrated to become the most amazing version of yourself when you are working hard to be present for a hurting place within you. You can do it better than anyone, given half a chance. And the "half a chance" part is the funniest part of all. Because most of us never give ourselves any chance at all to talk to our hurting selves on this level. And the ability to do it is right here, fully present, in every single moment of your life!

If you stop to really think about it, the act of putting the highest version of yourself in touch with the most needing places within you is genius. Who but you could really know EXACTLY what this Part needs, *if only you could see it clearly*—which you can't do when you are in battle with it, or trying to push it away, but which you *can* do when you see this Part through the loving lens of your Highest Self.

When the tug of war within shifts to *How can we work together?* what occurs is amazing, thrilling, sweet, tearful, way-clearing, and conversation-elevating. A new level of your own love, wisdom, and attunement gets to come forward—a level you were designed to have access to and which, under normal circumstances, you hardly ever even think to take out for a spin!

It's astonishing to see that such a thing is possible. And it's particularly poignant to realize that we have the capacity to "hold" the energy for ourselves—for a Part of ourselves—around a topic that, since this wound first took hold, no one has ever fully "held" for us before. Perhaps this is the most amazing truth of all:

For each ancient inner wound formed around you not getting what you expected or hungered for … you can meet yourself NOW.

YOUR TURN TO TRY IT: A JUMPING-IN POINT

I imagine I can hear you sitting out there in Book Reading Land now: *But how? Tell me exactly how.* And the funny thing is, I can't. But YOU *can.*

- I can help you conceive of the idea that such a conversation is possible (it is).
- I can tell you stories, give you examples, and offer you encouragement (you really, actually CAN dialogue with your Higher Self and with any other part of yourself, any time).
- I can tell you how to set it up (Higher Self and hurting self in two chairs).
- I can make suggestions about intentions to set (pitch your consciousness toward courage, clarity, healing) and what kind of "safe space" to create (curious, judgment-free).
- I can tell you how to recognize when you are hearing the voice of a Part (drama) or your Higher Self (loving).
- I can provide a SHIFT exercise at the end of this section (there is one) to offer up a clear point of entry and to highlight the fulcrum point of working with your inner voices.

But the moment you decide to enter in is, really, the moment I have been preparing you for. It's the one big core thing that only you can discover for yourself: *YOUR* "Herculean" moment. It's the moment in which *you turn to you* and invite a dialogue of a new sort—one of beautiful connection and communication *for you and within you.* I can help you, encourage you, cheer for you. But the truth of such a dialogue is that it must be all your own—yours to invite and yours to discover.

The "Herculean" effort it takes is really just a *s-t-r-r-e-t-c-h* that you choose to make *within yourself.*

It's you, turning away from numbing and drama-based distractions and facing the unknown, unexplored vast wilderness of the dialogues that are waiting to happen within you. It's you, realizing that such dialogues can be as healing, as tender, as uplifting, as encouraging, as revealing, and as cleansing as your consciousness is ready to allow.

The moment you enter in, curious and open to discovery, is *your* moment. Your gift to yourself. It's the gift you were born to give, when and if you choose to. It's a gift that exists out beyond doubt and second guessing, out beyond the normal flow of time itself—a moment that blooms only when you choose, consciously, to let it. You are in charge of whether or not a sea change begins to happen within you—of whether you do or do not become someone who has amazing and inspiring conversations on the inside. And you are in charge of whether that gorgeous kind of dialogue—evocative of the wonders of the Essence Level within and all around you—plays out every once in a great while, when things become utterly overwhelming and you are desperately out of options and ideas, or—or—OR, in an ongoing way, as an underlying aspect of Who You Now Are and how you are with yourself, on the inside.

The deepest healing comes not from the rare, desperate occasion of turning inward but from the reliability and familiarity of a luminous, expansive *ongoing* dialogue.

In a moment, you will turn to the PULSE SHIFT. You will give it a shot, I hope. You will open up a dialogue on the inside, poised to be expansive and good. And when you do, a place within you will be watching it all, working to make sense of what it is, how "real" it is—curious about who is speaking and how it all fits together. Dare to be a curious, open beginner. But, too, know that there are landmarks to watch for along the way. I can fortify you with them as you prepare to tap IN.

INNER DIALOGUE LANDMARKS

There are things that Parts *tend* to say when they are finally given an audience with our Higher Self. And there are things Higher Selves *tend* to communicate, verbally or non-verbally, in response. Those things often sound like variations on the following. I share them with you here in the spirit not of "feeding you lines" but rather exposing you to the sounds of a new inner language that is possible for you, *in your own way*. Yours won't sound exactly like this—yours will sound like YOU.

HURTING PARTS OFTEN COMMUNICATE:

- Why do I hurt so much? (or, Let me tell you why I hurt so much!)
- Is it safe for me to tell you my story?
- It's such a relief to share how I feel more fully.
- I feel so lonely/scared/forgotten/furious/weak.
- Is the inner job I have been doing obsolete? Appreciated? Does it still matter?
- If I stopped doing this job (protecting, hiding, etc.), what would I do instead?
- IN SHORT: Do you hear me? Will you help me?

HIGHER SELF OFTEN COMMUNICATES:

- I am listening with an open heart.
- It's safe for you to share the fullness of what you feel, in your own way, in your own voice.
- I can see how much pain you have been in.
- I am seeing the beauty of you, how hard you have been working, how much you care, the ways you may have been misunderstood.
- Are you open to sitting in silence together for a moment to make sure we are deeply aligned?
- The heart of what you are sharing seems to be ___. Does that feel accurate?
- I want to acknowledge you for your courage in sharing this.
- I see you.
- I am filled with love for you.
- I see a freer version of you very clearly, and I am holding that vision on your behalf.
- Are you open to exploring options for different ways of moving forward?
- IN SHORT: I hear you. I love you. I am here for you.

I have now seen and participated in hundreds of Higher Self/Hurting Part conversations made up of sentiments and communications much like these. These conversations tend to be relatively short in "real" time (perhaps five to fifteen minutes), though they cover great expanses in the shifts and expansions of the heart. And they tend to have an energetic "shape" as well. Certain hallmarks often appear.

A COMMON SHAPE OF HEALING CONVERSATIONS:

1. Anger or sadness growing larger and larger—a rush of communication and emotion
2. Eventually, deeper exhales, longer silences
3. An *unforeseeable* turn of the conversation that feels truer: more aligned, more connective
4. A new, more expansive view of the situation: options, ideas, and possibilities flowing forward
5. A lightness, an ease, optimism, and hope

The wonder of such exchanges is not the ways in which they all look the same, but rather the ways in which every single one, like snowflakes or DNA strands, is different and *unique*. Each one is uncannily, beautifully true to the Essence of Who YOU Are. In these two voices, you can begin to discover the language of your own healing and, out beyond healing, as we will see in Section 4, the language of your own self-expression and your ability to navigate, create, and *engage* going forward.

As all the many Parts within you become more oriented toward the voice of your Higher Self, an increasingly harmonious configuration of Parts can set in as a new default position. A kind of opening or conduit forms through which the energy of your Higher Self can easily, naturally flow, no longer working its way around the obstacles of a dispersed and disconnected system of Parts. What was a disjointed trickle of Higher Self energy can become a rightful, natural flow!

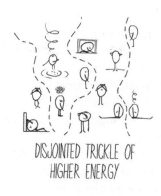

DISJOINTED TRICKLE OF
HIGHER ENERGY

HIGHER SELF ENERGY
FLOWING THROUGH

This is the shape of HEALING.

This is *deep inner alignment.* It's you, consciously evolving into a more connective, team-like configuration through attentive, loving dialogue and orientation.

It's a new level of inclusiveness that invites all under-exposed, under-valued, misunderstood, or "forgotten" Parts to step forward into the light of your own Higher Self. With such a configuration, deeper connections can form among *all* your Parts, while your Higher Self is rightfully restored to its natural state of ease and flow—not just invited into the conversation but allowed to become a centerpiece of your conscious well-being.

This kind of inner alignment *f-e-e-e-e-l-s s-o-o-o-o m-u-c-h b-e-t-t-e-r !*

It also "plays" better in the world, as the neediness, repetitiveness, blind spots, and dramas of random wounded Parts can dissipate within you, leaving you more open and oriented to the true depth of what is happening all around you.

Inner dialogues can shift out of stuck cycles. Troubled Parts can air and release their doubts and fears. Your Higher Self can respond with loving gifts of consciousness and *be heard.*

THE TRUTH IS ...

The truth is, you are strong enough.
The truth is, every place you have ever been has brought you exactly here.
The truth is, you are ready now for more.
The truth is, your inner light is resonant and healing.
The truth is, you are loved, surrounded by love, filled with love.
The truth is, all of your life challenges have been leading you somewhere
clearer, finer, and truer.
The truth is, you can stop hurting now and allow your burdens to transform.
The truth is, you are beautiful, full of life and light.
The truth is, you are not alone and never have been.
The truth of you is inside you, ready to flow outward,
touching you deeply and radiating out beyond you
to anyone who is ready to experience it with you.

As your Higher Voice is positioned to flow through you more and more, you will find more of what you have come to this book for—more of what you very likely came to this PLANET for: You will be operating and navigating from a Deeper YES within yourself.

And you don't need a spirituality degree or a guru or a year of meditative seclusion in order to begin. You need only to make one little SHIFT.

Chapter 20

YES Right Now: Takeaways & Explorations

Section 3, Deepen the Conversation Within, comes to a close with an offering of Key Takeaways and a SHIFT to help spark an ongoing dialogue with your Higher Self.

KEY TAKEAWAYS OF SECTION 3

1. **DIALOGUE WITHIN** – The quality of the dialogue playing out inside you matters deeply—both in terms of how conscious you are of it and how kind, curious, and loving it is in its nature. Tuning deeply inward to converse with yourself need not be a rare event. It can become *a way of being.* You can learn to be in an expansive and ongoing conversation with yourself that has the power to lift up your life, internally and externally.

2. **PARTS CONFIGURATIONS** – Deep within you are many Parts—many aspects or expressions of who you are. A healthy internal configuration of these Parts operates like a highly conscious and resourceful team, standing in a kind of inner circle, where all are connected and can interact with one another, and where key players can shift into the foreground and background in a beautifully coordinated orchestration, in direct alignment with your deepest desires. Trouble "out there in the world" on the Logistical Level occurs when Parts in an unhealthy configuration (less like a team and more like a noisy train station) act out, overly suppress themselves, or generally operate without clear and healthy connection to the other Parts within. All of this causes stuckness and trouble.

3. **CONFIGURATION STRENGTHENING** – You can improve the configuration of your Parts, and the flow of your well-being, by seeking

179

out groups with dynamics that mirror a healthy inner configuration and by engaging in flow-filled activities you feel called to engage in. You can set yourself up for doing transformative work on the inside by consciously, constructively venting any pressure built up from an unhealthy configuration. And you can set the stage for healing by learning to appreciate Peak Moments as a model for the way you want your configuration to operate and feel, more of the time.

4. **HEALING WOUNDED PARTS** – The most profound opportunity, though, lies in healing wounded Parts through inspired, loving, and purposeful dialogue, in four steps: (1) Calling all Parts, to announce your desire for a dialogue; (2) Tuning in to wounded Parts with an open heart; (3) Deepening your capacity to "hold" the energy of an upset Part without trying to manage the outcome; and (4) Responding with a judgment-free YES Orientation toward whatever your wounded Parts have to share. This is the essence of healing and can be a real turning point for well-being.

5. **YOUR HIGHER SELF** – There is within you a specific concentration of energies that is your Higher Self: Essence Level radiance, wisdom, clarity, and expansive thinking, all available to you any time you intentionally turn inward and summon it. What keeps most of us from accessing this place is that we forget we have the power to do so. But it is always present, and, unlike Parts, it is unencumbered by drama, wounds, doubt, or resistance. It is quite simply **the Finest, Truest place within you.**

6. **TWO CHAIRS: BOOM!** – You can use two dialogue chairs to separate out a hurting Part from the rest of you, freeing YOU up to experience *reality without that wound*, and freeing the "wound"/wounded Part to speak openly and to feel truly heard by you, perhaps for the first time ever. You can powerfully heighten that experience by putting your *Higher Self* in one chair and a wounded Part in the other. BOOM! This brings the greatest concentration of your own love and clarity directly to the most hurting place within you! You can offer, to yourself, the love and attention you most needed (and didn't get) when the wound was initially formed. The results are powerful, freeing, and full of unexpected twists and wonders. A deeper resonance—a Deeper YES—can ripple forward. And you? You can feel better, and better, and BETTER with each successive dialogue.

TRY THIS: THE PULSE SHIFT

We have looked at a total of seven steps for deepening your inner dialogue. You may or may not choose to follow each one. I share these primarily because I think it can be powerful for your consciousness to begin to realize such steps exist. That said, to whatever degree you decide to explore them yourself, please do. And if you want to simply amalgamate all of the Section 3 principles and try one simple exercise, try the Pulse SHIFT.

This SHIFT is very simple. It's based on the idea that access to your Higher Self is always just one conscious SHIFT away from wherever you are right now. This SHIFT helps you send a *pulsing* energy of gratitude and invitation directly to your Higher Self, whenever it occurs to you to do so.

You now have many reasons to "listen to yourself" and "talk to yourself" on a whole new level. The desire is likely in place, as are numerous suggestions for what helps and examples of how things might sound when you put a struggling Part in one chair and your Higher Self in the other. With all of this lined up, all should be well. But the simple fact of the matter is that even people who know about Higher Self inner dialogue and have had amazing experiences with it themselves don't go "IN" on this deeper level as often as you might think, or as often as they might wish, or might benefit from.

I am generally flabbergasted at the magnificence of what people can call forward—clients, myself, individuals I've seen in workshops—once they are "IN" and giving voice to their Higher Self. But I am equally astonished at how *infrequently* these same people actually DO IT—actually take a moment to *TUNE IN*.

I believe the way of addressing all these lost opportunities to turn inward lies in having access to a PULSE SHIFT—a little "assist" right at the critical energetic tipping point when you need it most. It can make such a difference to have one tiny extra boost of intentionality and permission right in the exact moment you become aware you want to access your Higher Self and are perhaps about to resist doing so. This SHIFT is all about infusing one simple question into *any* moment when it occurs to you that you might want to TUNE IN. It's about activating this SHIFT *before* that notion can morph into a big deal or an opportunity to distract yourself or build up resistance. This SHIFT opens the door of dialogue, any time, all the time, in a purposeful, specific, and, hopefully, inviting way.

THE PULSE SHIFT:
5 STEPS FOR DEEPENING THE DIALOGUE

Try this SHIFT whenever you want a Higher Self connection.

1. **Breathe Deeply** – Close your eyes and take several deep, centering breaths, letting it dawn on you that you are fully intentional about tuning in to your Higher Self and tapping in to those powers.

2. **Pulse Positivity Inward** – Begin pulsing energy inward in waves, starting small and building in depth and fullness. Focus this pulsing directly toward your Higher Self, speaking the language of deep gratitude and boundless love with the energy you send in. Let yourself feel how powerful it is to send loving energy inward to this place within you that is usually all about sending love outward. Feel the conscious connection come alive.

3. **Identify a Topic** – Without fanfare, straightforwardly ask your Higher Self what topic you would be best served by focusing on right now (an upset, a new interest, a relationship, a confusion, a goal). Sit silently and wait. Trust whatever comes forward in your consciousness even if it's different than what you think it "should" be. (If you are challenged by this, let yourself see a row of possible topics and wait to see which one "glows" differently from the others.)

4. **Ask for Learning** – Ask your Higher Self, "What ONE THING is it time for me to understand in a new way, just now, about this topic?"

5. **Receive a New Awareness** – State aloud, "I am ready to receive your response," which may be a word, image, phrase, or something else entirely. Clear a space within yourself and assume that whatever comes forward is sacred and carefully attuned exactly to the level of resonance and authenticity you are ready for now. State your understanding out loud so you can hear your own clarity.

Simple Alternatives – If you want a simpler way of getting acquainted with your Higher Self, try asking, with an open and trusting heart, for guidance on tiny things. If you are out for a solo walk, ask your Higher Self, "How many minutes should I walk for, for my own highest good?" Don't try to *think* of the answer—just listen for an awareness coming from deep within you and go with it. Honor the response you get, to the minute. You can try this with "What should I do to relax right now?" or "Which route should I take home?" or "What should I say when I first see my daughter tonight?" I always complete such requests with the phrase, "for the highest good of all concerned." The goal is not to "guess" the right answer, any more than it is to "prove the answer wrong" (these energies and orientations don't help with your goal of strengthening your connection to your Higher Self). The opportunity here is simply to locate a place within you that has your highest good and the highest good of all concerned in mind, and then to lean into bringing that particular "advice" (awareness) to life, being open to discovering, "How is this answer amazing? What does this particular answer allow for, free me up for, make possible?"

What we are really doing with this SHIFT practice is clearing a regular, ongoing, "pulsing" kind of communication pathway between (a) your ability to consciously reach inward and (b) your Higher Self's supreme ability to reach out toward you with assistance, *when invited.*

This practice, which you can do ten times a day, if you like (at a stoplight, in your bathroom, as you wait in line), can become as natural as breathing. It can, itself, become a new kind of pulsing momentum informing all the meaningful twists and turns of your life. (For which topic, actually, would you prefer *not* to have the counsel of your wisest, most loving, and most far-seeing self?)

Over time, as you become engaged regularly in more flowing Higher Self conversations, a deep inner glow and radiance will likely become more consistent within you; situations that previously would have felt triggering or overwhelming may feel like part of something larger from which you can learn and grow. You will likely experience more inner peace and more exuberance in connecting with the world around you. In short, the more you dialogue in this way, the more you get to walk the earth with the newfound confidence that comes from knowing your Higher Self has your back!

Part of the strength of this practice is your willingness to hear and connect with whatever knowingness breaks through the static of your inner, ongoing "noise," even if it seems like a whisper or a fleeting little jolt. And to receive whatever you get with an open heart and curious, trusting mind. In the beginning, if one in five of these "Higher Self conversations" is helpful in a way you can directly understand and apply, that's still a LOT more than what was happening before you started tuning in.

Best of all, such conversations are the cornerstone for this last piece we are going to look at together: the process of navigating your life from deeper within your own internal YES.

SECTION 4

NAVIGATE THE DEEPER YES

YOU IN MOTION

"It doesn't interest me how old you are.
I want to know if you will risk looking like a fool for love,
for your dream, for the adventure of being alive.

It doesn't interest me what planets are squaring
your moon … I want to know if you have touched
the centre of your own sorrow,
if you have been opened by life's betrayals,
or have become shriveled and closed
from fear of further pain.

I want to know if you can sit with pain, mine or your own …
if you can dance with wildness and
let the ecstasy fill you to the
tips of your fingers and toes … .

I want to know if you can see Beauty even when it is
not pretty every day. … I want to know if you can live
with failure, yours and mine, and still stand at the edge
of the lake and shout to the silver of the full moon,

"YES."

—Oriah Mountain Dreamer

In this Section ...

I want to remind you
that each moment
within a life
is a brand-new invitation to
NAVIGATE,
from deeper within yourself,
toward that which
FEELS GOOD.

I want to show you
how to ask the bigger questions,
lean into your next step,
and invite new possibilities
wherever you go.

Chapter 21

Putting It All Together

Ultimately, Living the Deeper YES means giving yourself the *inner freedom* and *inner permission* to navigate at a higher (more awake) frequency, over and over again. And to do so in ways that carry you to places that feel good, at the deepest levels, in ways that help you learn and expand, instead of struggling or shutting down.

I want to help you pull together the three key considerations we've looked at, so you can gather the best of what is here and use it to move forward into a truer, finer version of yourself. I want to do this not because you (or I, or anyone) is likely to achieve full-on, flowing fine-ness every moment. But rather because experiencing more of it is *possible*. And because living that way more of the time feels better.

When I started to more fully honor *Who I Really Am*, in my actions and in my choices, I began seeing and experiencing a new level of wonderment around me and within me. I found that I became more magnetic to coincidences, intimacy, and love. I started making choices from a different place inside of myself—a place within me that was deeper, not reacting and responding, but guiding my movements at my own natural, true pacing, and operating more and more from *that* pacing, instead of the pacing of others. Twenty years ago my life shifted onto a fresher course that was, and is, less trapped-feeling, more playful, surprising, ease-filled, and satisfying, much more of the time. And, importantly, I began finding it natural and joyful to assist others who wanted help in opening up to more of this in their own lives.

All of this happened not just because I knew more, understood more, and began listening more deeply within and around me, but also because *I started navigating differently*.

I invite you to look at the practice of navigating one moment to the next, in a more conscious way, so you can lead yourself into a life you love. As valuable as it is to achieve a clear understanding of Essence Level energy (Section 1), the freedoms that lie out beyond the distractions of inner and outer drama (Section 2), and the synchronicity of a harmonious inner team of Parts (Section 3), life gets very real when we bring these new *conceptual* awarenesses into the *reality* of our everyday navigations.

Let's discuss and celebrate what is possible *when you navigate more consciously.* It's simple, really. We've been on a journey together to consider the deeper aspects of three ideas. When we put them together, they tell a powerful story of what it can mean for you to come alive in your own life in ways that feel more attuned, more "at agency," *and*, simultaneously, more carried and supported by a larger flow.

Section 1: Shift the Balance

There is Essence Level energy all around you. You can tap into it (*wonders!*) *or* you can fight against it (*struggle and stress*). The choice is before you literally every moment. Opening up to your awareness of Essence energy means choosing YES to the wonders of the greater context in which you live, more and more of the time.

Section 2: Change Your Mind

The dramas in your life can either be upsetting, wound-feeding, repetitive distractions OR bright waving flags letting you know that it's time to turn inward to deepen and clarify your connection with yourself. Turning inward versus turning accusingly outward at moments of upset means choosing YES to more of what is possible in the inner workings of YOU.

Section 3: Deepen the Conversation Within

When you turn toward the places within you that are filled with pain, or whispering of wisdom, you do so either with curiosity, love, and intentionality *or* with judgment, frustration, and distrust. Turning inward lovingly, on an ongoing basis, allows for a cosmic kind of internal reconfiguring, in which damaged Parts can relax, feel seen, and shrink back down to a more natural size. And your Higher Self can be heard more audibly and therefore relied on more explicitly for guidance. Turning inward lovingly means saying YES to *all* of your Parts, to the formation of a new inner harmony, and, ultimately, saying YES to that powerful and loving presence that is and always has been your amazing Higher Self.

Navigating the Deeper YES means embracing this three-part understanding as you move forward in the way that you make choices, chart your course, and make sense of what is happening around you.

Navigating consciously means inviting your deeper, truer energies to come into alignment with the larger energies all around you.

As we saw in Section 3, trying to invite that kind of alignment *in the absence of harmonious inner voices* is a formula for frustration, resistance, chaos, confusion, and disappointment. It's too soon to try to make things happen "out there" in the world if you are avoiding making things happen within your own heart, among all the Parts of Who You Are. But once you begin to prioritize that, to tune inward, and to care deeply about what you are hearing from the voices within, the time becomes ripe to align your outward orientation—your real-world choices, your larger goals, your minute-to-minute decisions—with a larger flow.

Inviting alignment with a Deeper YES connection to all the voices within yourself creates a fertile, energetic environment for coincidence, flow, serendipity, and the ability to open to what feels good. At that point, and not before, having some tips for navigation can make all the difference.

Chapter 22

Tips for Navigation

Navigating a life is no small thing.

It's the big direction you are headed in, and have been, for decades, whether you've been conscious you've been heading in a direction or not. It's the way you respond to the tugs and pulls of whimsy, happenstance, addiction, fear, and blind luck. It's those moments of reckoning, like mine, or Rose's, in the shock of her breakup: "waking up" and discovering that somehow you have drifted *f-a-a-a-a-r* off course from where you thought you were and where you intended to be—*f-a-a-a-a-r* from what once felt good but, if you are honest with yourself, no longer really still does. On a scale much closer in, it's your goals for the year, your hopes for that large project you're embarking on, your wishes for the week, or even the hour that lies ahead of you.

But more than anything else, it's the degree to which you are awake and inviting something deeply aligned with the best version of yourself that feels good—in the moment *and* in the overall direction in which it's pointing you and your future.

What if the minute-to-minute act of navigating a life were broken down into something simple, graspable, and YES-able? I don't want to pretend I can offer you an infallible approach. But I do love the idea of getting concrete with you, in four guiding Basic Encouragements that look like this:

1. **Readiness**
2. **Movement**
3. **Course Attunement**
4. **Joy**

Before I give these Basic Encouragements the kind of dimension they'll need in order to be valuable to you, I want to invite you to stop and make a conscious decision to hear them from the place of lowest resistance and most heightened curiosity you are able to access. Whether you are always fully aware of it or not, you are the gatekeeper not only of what gets into your consciousness, but also *how it is greeted when it enters.*

Maybe these Basic Encouragements can't make much difference for you. But *maybe they can.* And maybe what stands between them—or any healthy, self-supporting tools—and you, marveling at how much better things are going, is your willingness to hear them from a place of wonder, hope, creativity, and open-armed greeting.

The first time I ever went to see a professional intuitive, I spent two days just opening myself up, more and more, trusting the great reputation she had, and asking the Universe and myself over and over again, *Please— crack me open <u>enough</u> so that what she has to offer can really impact me.* I made the ground within myself ripe and fertile because I knew I was strong enough to do exactly that, simply by *choosing* it. What that intuitive had to say landed in me in a place that was incredibly willing to grow, to see, to let what she offered soften me, expand me, and loosen up the tight places so I could breathe and feel more deeply again. *She* was awesome—talented, attuned, uncannily wise. But it was I who really let her awesomeness *in*, where it could do the most good.

You can do that any time, and I invite you to do it now. It's important to trust the person who is reaching out the hand to help you before you take their help. And I hope you trust me by now. My intentions are good. But more to the point, I invite you to trust YOU. You are *sooooo* powerful that you can *choose* to make the receptive ground within you fertile, right now. And in so doing, you will get even more out of what you are about to read.

Invite the stillness. Set down the book. Take a breath. For real. Encourage your most fertile receptors to rise up and come forward, to open, before you continue reading: *I want to learn to navigate in a truer fashion,* you can tell yourself, *and I am willing to let what I am about to read penetrate, touch me, and help me grow.* Give yourself a moment to try this now.

That's what navigation is, really. It's daring to grow in a direction that lines up with Who You Most Deeply Are.

I am imagining I feel you deepening, now. And I am acknowledging you for doing so. It's a very loving gift to yourself. Let's look at the four Basic Encouragements one at a time.

1. Readiness: Ask a Higher Question

Deep navigation is less about responding and more about asking. It's about daring to put your feelers out and grope around a little, rather than just sitting still and hoping. And, most specifically, it's about asking a certain *kind* of question—one that stems from exactly where you are and then invites you to take one stretch further. When this happens enough times, momentum starts to kick in, coincidences start to happen, and you find yourself in the flow.

So, what might you ask?

In my experience, the most pure and powerful navigations occur when you identify an area where you feel desire—hunger, interest, curiosity, wanting—and then you ask a "Higher Question" of a "Higher Energy." Get inspired by the Pulse SHIFT (#3) and ask your Higher Self. Ask the Universe. Ask anything or anyone or any energy you are aware of that feels like it vibrates on a higher frequency—angels, God, nature, a wise departed loved one, whatever you are drawn to. Ask this question, specifically:

What am I finally ready to know and understand, right now, about the thing or situation I currently desire?

This question, if you let it be, can be surprisingly powerful. It's the lightning bolt of you, identifying an area of wanting, lacking, wishing, and, instead of trying to "conjure" some "solution" in the physical world, simply inviting the expansion of your own consciousness *as it relates to this topic.*

When I am asking this question, I am *REALLY ASKING*—often literally or emotionally—"on my knees." I'm asking with profound curiosity. It's not a half-hearted undertaking. I am asking with the assumption that there actually is something my consciousness has *genuinely not taken in*—yet. Something that is holding me back from seeing more clearly and navigating more directly toward that which feels good. It takes a lot of conscious intention to position yourself in the place of *really asking* this kind of a Higher Question. But when you do, look out.

When I'm asking this question, what I am really saying is, *Given that I am ready to grow, what is it now time for me to ... let go of more completely OR embrace more fully; to take more lightly OR take more seriously; to feel more deeply OR protect myself from more completely; to understand, share, or appreciate more thoroughly? What is it time for, right now, in regard to this desire, and my consciousness and growth? If something within me were willing to soften and shift to accommodate some new understanding, what would that understanding be?*

And what I am really coming to grips with, in being able to ask such a question (and let its answer *touch me*, rather than irritate me or bounce off of me), is some needed shift within myself that will allow me to feel more of what I long to feel. It's not the car I want, really, or the house or the job—it's the way I imagine those things are going to allow me to *feel*—more engaged, more empowered, more secure, perhaps. This kind of Higher Question comes from someplace different than simply, "*I want this—can I please have it?*" It cuts right to the place inside you where your own limitations might be holding you back, and asks what kind of an inner shift it is time for, and what, specifically, it is time for you to know, in order for you to FEEL more of whatever it is you imagine that new car or house or job will allow you to feel.

This question could, of course, be thrown out challengingly—the way I COULD have gone to see that intuitive I visited (*If you're so tapped in, then what's the name of my cat, huh?!*). But it can also be posed with humility and great readiness to take in something new, and to let that new understanding change you. When I ask this kind of Higher Question, I accompany it with the deepest form of willingness I know how to conjure. I say:

I am ready, now, to hear this answer, in whatever form it arrives.

2. Movement: Lean in the Golden Direction

Once this kind of question has been posed, one of two things will happen. Either you will get some immediate response—some discernable, recognizably clear inner voice or outer sign about how to proceed—or you won't. I love it when I pose a Higher Question and can feel in my bones right away that I am receiving a clear answer in the form of a coincidence, sign, or "knowing" that comes over me as I sit with the question. And this does happen, more than I ever would have guessed back when I was living a smaller, tighter, more muzzled and muffled inner life. Back when I wasn't walking around posing Higher Questions and believing that guiding answers would come.

That said, as often as not, I don't immediately get a perfectly clear "response," "knowing," or meaningful sign, and you may not either, especially in the beginning. In the past, posing a Higher Question and "not getting an answer" would have frustrated me, set me to doubting, or stopped me in my tracks. But these days, I know what a difference it makes to *keep moving anyway*—to choose a direction and keep leaning forward.

At USM they shared with us, in situation after stymying situation, this curious and powerful offering: "Spirit meets you at the point of action."

This is a concept I now pass along with great encouragement to others. It's like a quiet song, playing encouragingly in the back of my head, in the back of the room, helping us all to remember that the wonders, the connections, and the coincidences don't tend to happen when we are sitting still. They come alive and dance along with us when we are in motion. We become more "find-able" by the flowing energies of the Universe when we move about, infusing our ideas and dreams with the energy of motion.

We invite more flow
when we *become* flow, ourselves.

Even the disjointed, awkward first steps of movement (when we lean into them instead of holding ourselves back) begin to attract something newer and finer.

The direction of our motion *does* matter. When navigating, it's preferable to intentionally point yourself toward that which feels most rightful, hopeful, or meaningful. But it's the motion itself, even more than the direction we are pointed in, that really matters, I keep finding. With an open heart and a willingness to grow and see more clearly, all roads lead to healing and fruition: We dare to engage in stillness to allow for the knowing, and then we dare to step into motion, to bring that knowing to life.

Which way should I point myself, though?, you may ask. I can't always tell which direction feels most rightful, hopeful, or meaningful. Moving for the sake of moving feels strange, like a waste of energy, like it could quickly steer me in problematic directions.

I try to point, and help point others, always, in what I call the Golden Direction. If you are standing there, looking at all the different ways you could go in any given moment *(Should I tell her I am upset or keep it to myself? Should I marry him or not? Should I join them on their walk, stay home and do my work, watch TV, meditate?)*, you might be able to see two choices or you might be able to see a hundred variations on moving forward. Regardless of how many you see, I have discovered that *one* of them will always "shimmer" a bit more than the others, if you let yourself feel your way into it.

I try always to move, even just a tiny little bit, in that Golden Direction. It's like closing my eyes and daring to imagine I can tell which option shines even just a little bit brighter—believing that I have the power to actually discern it, and finding that, when I believe I have the power, I DO!

It never ceases to amaze me how, when I reach a juncture like this with a client, about any kind of decision they are trying to make, if I ask them which option is "shimmering" a little more than the others, they discover they *know the answer* to this odd (Higher) question. Without my even necessarily explaining what I mean by "shimmering," they get the gist of my question and, when they quiet themselves for a moment, find they are capable of answering it, usually surprising themselves in the process. Identifying which direction is "shimmery" doesn't necessarily mean they are ready to *move* in that direction (resistance can be a powerful thing). But it does mean that people seem to *know*, when you ask them—when you give them even half a chance—which option seems to be "more special, more amazing, more magical, more Golden," if even by just a tiny fraction more than the others.

And, rest assured, moving—in ANY direction—invites more energy, more data, more motion, and therefore more clarity. The less sure I feel about what, exactly, the Golden Direction is, the more I make small movements, ones I could reverse if I wanted to, but which keep me in motion all the same.

Each little step I take means that I am navigating forward into the unknown. I have to learn to develop some kind of trust of my own knowing, about where the "shimmer" of the Golden Direction might lie, and how the Universe might help point me there. So, I start to listen *differently*. I listen not as if the Universe is silent, or as if it is conspiring against me. I listen *as if the Universe loves me.*

Listen as if the Universe Loves You.

I listen as if it has been speaking to me all along—as if every turn of a branch in the wind, every billboard, every honking car, every unexpected email, every funny little coincidence, fleeting magical feeling, or unique bird has been here all along to help me see and understand something new about the journey I am on. And, I find, when I listen that way, I feel clearer, "connect more dots," and take better, more wide-awake guesses about how the Universe and I might be in dialogue and how the events and "signposts" around me might be helping me along, if only I will see it—helping me deepen my connection with my own inner knowingness, and willingness to find assistance along the way, in its many glorious and serendipitous forms.

Waking up to the fullness of your life means grappling with the idea that all of us are, in fact, always in dialogue with that higher-frequency place within us and around us—always asking questions and receiving answers—whether we are conscious of it or not. And that joy and fulfillment—a deeper kind of YES—come from learning to make that dialogue conscious, invited, and part of your everyday navigational choices. In the aftermath of having consciously posed a Higher Question like this, we have expanded our own awareness of and interest in the voices within and around us, because we have decided we are ready to *know more.*

I invite you to put out a question—not about the "thing you want" but about the expansion of understanding you are ready to make. Then stay alert for the answers all around you. There are magnificent conversations to be had. Your answers are everywhere.

3. Course Attunement: Follow the Shiver

So now you have located a topic. You have translated whatever it is you don't yet have or know into a Higher Question around that topic, and you are moving in the most "Golden" direction you can identify. Good. But navigation is not about simply picking a direction (however shimmering and "Golden" it might seem) and blindly trudging forward in a straight line. It's a million little choices and decisions, subtle and gigantic, moment by moment, that alter and inform your course as new data comes in. And this is where your physical body—glorious divining rod that it is—comes into play.

One very helpful thing to know as you navigate is this:

Your body doesn't lie.
It will always let you know
what you most need to know.

Your body will always let you know in one way or another (increase in back pain, stomach ache, headache, sharp uptick in fatigue, general "off" feeling) when a maneuver you have made is divergent from the deeper truth of Who You Are. And that same body can consistently be counted on to offer you an expanded sense of well-being (long deep exhale, relaxation of the shoulders, a lifting of tension in the face, an urge to giggle or laugh, watering of the eyes) when the path you are walking is deeply rightful. The "organs of communication" vary from person to person, but learning the language of the way your body communicates with you can make a powerful difference in navigating even the simplest of choices.

I have found that I experience something like a "shiver" when I am on a rightful track, meaning, when I am not just superficially enjoying a playful distraction but truly moving forward in a way that radiates joy from someplace deep within me—a stirring of that deeper YES. For me, this kind of shiver feels like a little ripple, moving under my skin in a subtle, magical, fleeting little way.

"Follow the shiver," I say to my clients, meaning, *Whatever it is for you— shiver, watering eyes, tingling up your spine*—notice that your body is talking to you about joy, and trust that it knows and can help you navigate, much more than you previously realized was possible. Your body knows how to discern a higher vibration from a lower one. It knows when it is in alignment with the energies around you.

If you are in a room with others and feeling clenched, or stiff, or like you have to clamp some part of yourself down to fit in, notice what is happening with your body and become playful with any choice you might make, even a minuscule one (breathe deeper, move to the other side of the room, make physical contact with someone present, give yourself permission to step out of the space for a moment to "make a phone call"). Do something small but meaningful to shift the way you are sliding through this moment—to navigate a tiny (but meaningful) bit differently.

When we stop using the events around us to "determine" how to feel, we begin to wake up to the subtleties of what our body knows, and can guide us through. Ask yourself: *Once I have set a course, how often do I stop to check in along the way? How often do I dare to see how my body is holding up along the course? To ask what it might be telling me? To offer breaks long enough to gather new and better data about my course? And then to resume my movement, where I can put myself back into a flow and learn yet more?*

Your life—the moments large and small that comprise the journey you are on—is an opportunity to attune on many levels, and get much better data about what works, what feels good, what distracts you temporarily (nothing wrong with that, on occasion—a little fun and respite along the way can be a beautiful thing), and, most importantly, what feeds you deeply.

I invite you to "know" better—to take better cues all around and within you—about what feeds you deeply, and what puts your body into an authentic state of goodness. And that means, as we come 'round the bend to the completion of our time together, an appreciation for the incredible navigational power of joy.

4. Joy: The Final Invitation

I want to leave you with the very thing I offered up to you when first we met: an Invitation.

I want to invite you to make invitations of your own, wherever you go.

Invitations to the voices within you—the shy voices that have been hesitant to speak up, the wise ones that can get drowned out, and the voices within you that deeply know the language of joy and are perfectly equipped to help lead you there, if you will let them.

Invitations to the energies around you: You have the power to dip your consciousness into the Essence Level and invite something amazing to play out, not just once in a while, but again and again, everywhere you navigate. The more you orient yourself toward this, the more likely you are to see the wonder-filled moments that are occurring, all around you, all the time.

Invitations to others: You have the power, too, to live as a fuller version of yourself. By doing simply this, you will be inviting others who are touched by your presence to rise to a new level of authenticity and fullness themselves.

We live in a Universe that is all about love and possibility. Sometimes there are twists and turns that soften and expand us if we dare to let them. But the predominant direction of flow is toward love, caring, and possibility. More than any other single thing, this flow—this onward, expansive, ever-present Essence Level flow—is about joy. Finding your way forward is not, ultimately, about a step, a task, or an exercise, though I have done what I can here to break down what I've discovered in ways that I hope might help inform your journey.

Finding your way forward is about a knowing, deep within you, that you were always MEANT to dance with the energies around you. It's about knowing that the peaceful, brilliant, and beautiful path before you was always MEANT to broaden and fill with joy in any and every moment where you dare to step forward fully, wholly, ready to ask, ready to receive, present to the alchemy of you and this world: meeting, clashing, informing, shifting, and resonating into something fuller, finer, truer.

Invite something amazing to happen for you, in this moment. In the next moment. In your most vibrant, connected moments and in your darkest, most devastatingly isolated ones as well.

I am here to encourage you to invite it, to allow it—to hear your own life in its fullest resonance: a giant sustainable gong that says, resonantly, repeatedly, bravely, sweetly … YES.

Acknowledgments

Except for the times when it felt ridiculously hard for a few terrifying moments here and there, writing this book was a joyfully uplifting experience for me. This is largely because I was never, ever doing it alone. My sister, Amy, was my original cheerleader. I would send her early chapters, she would write back, "Wow! Holy crap! Keep going!" and I was on my way. Thanks to my many early readers for your encouragement, ideas, skillful delivery of constructive criticism, and for believing in me and saying so: Amy, Allison, Matteo, Caitlin, Kristin, Jimmy, Keith, Szifra, Beth, Nancy, Liz, and, of course, Mom.

Thanks very especially to Virginia Fitzgerald, who did all the illustrations for this book, listening carefully, squiggling playfully, and crafting images that made me smile. Thanks to Keith for your warm heart, your generous availability, your lightening skills, and for staying close. And thanks to Allison for innumerable incredibly inspired edits and encouragements.

Doug Stone not only wrote the Foreword to this book (in addition to co-authoring one of Penguin's best-selling books ever—*Difficult Conversations*—wow!), but he also checked in with me, encouraged me, mentored me, and sat out on my back deck every several months to ask how it was going, *actually listening* in a very real way as I prattled on. Thank you, Doug, for being present at all the meaningful junctures, and for caring and saying so. Thank you, too, for the powerful and transformative work you do in the world, and for the way your book has changed the landscape of dialogue around the whole freaking *planet*. Finally, thank you for a Foreword so marvelous it made me scream out loud in my office the first time I read it. Jim came running up the stairs to see if a pig had been slaughtered, but it was just me, as happy a Foreword reader as ever there was.

My developmental editor, Rebecca at KN Literary Arts, appeared magically out of the ethers with a steady hand, a gentle but clear vision, and a wonderful way of finding big chunks I could cut to save the rest of the universe from having to read an eight-million-word book. I felt steadied, encouraged, and appreciated from beginning to end. Thank you, Rebecca.

A very special message of appreciation and heartfelt gratitude goes out to my gurus, Drs. Ron and Mary Hulnick of the University of Santa Monica. Watching Ron translate ideas into drawings changed my life in a profound and lasting way, and learning how to grow in the presence of Mary's loving energy awakened my heart. USM was the springboard from which I realized I could choose to create a more conscious and loving life than the one I had.

This book came into being largely because I won a Hay House Publishing contest! Upon winning, I discovered a powerful support system in my two supposed "competitors"—Nancy Mae (author of *The Energetic Fertility Method*) and Mary Shores (author of *Conscious Communications*). They were the other two winners of the contest and, perhaps improbably, we became a regular and affirming support system for one another along the way.

Thank you, Twinkle, for making me a real writer by publishing my dune buggy story in your book, *Women of Spirit: Exploring Sacred Paths of Wisdom Keepers*. And thank you most especially for your wild inspiration of inviting me to s*ing* as part of my TEDx Talk! (*what?!*) That idea and experience woke something up in me and set me on this whole new, joyful book-talk-with-singing path!

An unusually special thank you to all the members of Make Stuff Up University (MSUU), past and present, for offering your unique contributions in a loving, caring, conscious community where I could test my theories, keep opening and re-opening my heart, and dare to say, "I feel daunted, but I really want to write a book!" Thanks especially to the five members of my MSUU project team who provided such expansive encouragement as I found my voice and kept celebrating and refining my message until it materialized: Allison, Kristin, Wendy, Jody, and Kris.

Thank you to my strong, beautiful, all-knowing mom, and to my cosmic-thinking, daughter-adoring, eternally sweet dad, who died during the time I was writing this book. You both told me every day with your words, with the way you looked into my eyes, and with your strong presence in my life that I am loved. With your hearts wide open, this past year in particular, the two of you taught me what it means to go the distance.

Chris walked with me almost every week, and never failed to ask how things were going with the book. Jan sent me a bouquet of roses when I completed my first NaNoWriMo draft in record time. Greg cheered me on, served as a writing buddy, and offered up helpful advice and contacts along the way.

Thank you to the following people for offering well-timed words of wisdom or encouragement at the exact moment I needed them most: my brother Al, Doug H., Kristin B., Erica, Sheila H., Sheila M., Amy F., Rev. Jim., Miles K., Wendy C., Carrie, Eric K., Tony S., Dr. David T, Robin, Rich B, Jay, Mary C., and a guiding force in my life, Dr. Norm.

Angela, I stand in awe of your generosity, your tenderness of spirit, and the way you somehow just materialized as a shining, USM-infused beacon at the midpoint and again at the completion point of my book. You lifted my hopes with your enthusiasm for the content, and later cheered me exuberantly across the finish line while polishing off all those final grammar edits. You are the angel of my book, and I am lucky and grateful.

Thank you, Heather at Balboa Press, for your steadfast and professional assistance in turning the blinky, backlit manuscript on my laptop into a thing of beauty with a cover and actual pages that I can flip and flap and flaunt and fling with joy.

My son Ben screamed *super* loud and jumped up and down hugging me in the front hallway one day when he came home from school and I triumphantly showed him the first finished manuscript printout. When I shared doubts that real publication would ever come to fruition, my son Sam lovingly raised the question, "Why are you worrying about this? You KNOW it's going to happen." Both of my sons learned to cook and took up a huge share of that task so I could write. So now we have not only a finished book but also a house full of gourmet chefs (seriously!) to boot. How cool is that? Thank you, Ben and Sam, for your cheers and for believing in me.

And thanks most especially of all to my sweet husband, Jim, for everything, everything, everything. Loving you has been one of the great privileges and joys of my lifetime. Many people gave me book feedback, but yours read like a love letter, one I will cherish always, as I do you.

About the Musical Album

The Days of Your Opening is a collection of original songs by Anna Huckabee Tull celebrating the foundational messages of *Living the Deeper YES.*

It is available at CDBaby.com, iTunes, Amazon, and hundreds of other digital and streaming sites.

See also Anna's other albums:
Open Now – Autobiographical
Other People's Stories – Commissioned Songs
Love All Over the Place – A Study of Four Distinct Phases of Love
Every Day – Songs in Celebration of Parents and Children, Young and Grown

About the Author

Phil Harkins Photography

Anna Huckabee Tull is a Master Life Coach of twenty years and an award-winning Singer-Songwriter with more than 250 commissioned works created for individuals all over the globe. She received her Master's in Spiritual Psychology from the University of Santa Monica while simultaneously attending the Harvard Divinity School. In 2008, she founded Make Stuff Up University, helping individuals become intentional about creating a life that aligns with their deeper desires and offerings.

This is Anna's first book, timed for simultaneous release with her fifth national album, *The Days of Your Opening*, a collection of songs celebrating the foundational messages from *Living the Deeper YES.*

Anna's lifetime study of the dynamics of Stuckness and Flow has taken her to the offices of CEOs and White House executives, into the homes of budding entrepreneurs and pioneers, and behind the walls of prisons and psych wards where she teaches and performs. She lives in a light-filled house in the woods of Concord, Massachusetts, with three excellent humans: her husband and two teenage sons. She has spent a good chunk of the past year walking every single street in her hometown.